Control and Chaos

John Shenton

Published by John Shenton, 2024.

While every precaution has been taken in the preparation of this book, the publisher assumes no responsibility for errors or omissions, or for damages resulting from the use of the information contained herein.

CONTROL AND CHAOS

First edition. October 1, 2024.

ISBN: 979-8227550958

Written by John Shenton.

Also by John Shenton

Business Plan Basics
The Bahamas - More Islands and Recipes Than You Expect!
Collected Musings from Bricks and Mortar to E-commerce
The Smart City Odyssey: Unveiling the Secrets to Traveller-Centric
Software
The Dragon's Gambit: China's Bid for Global Dominance and the
Western Response
Silent Weapon
Business Basics: Money Sources
Influx
Fried Chips
Mandates, Motors, and Misinformation
Echos of Orwell
Control and Chaos
The Empire's Warning: What Rome's Fall Tells Us About the West
Today

Table of Contents

Foreword

The rapid shift towards a cashless society is no longer a distant possibility but an imminent reality, as governments and financial institutions worldwide race to explore the potential of Central Bank Digital Currencies (CBDCs). In this book, *Control and Chaos: The Perils and Pitfalls of a Cashless Future*, I have undertaken the task of examining the multifaceted consequences of this transformation. The evolution of money, as outlined in Chapter 1, reflects a relentless march toward greater convenience and efficiency, yet it also harbours significant risks that demand scrutiny and robust debate.

We are living in an era where the rise of digital currencies has forced central banks and governments to reconsider the very nature of money. From China's Digital Yuan to the European Union's exploration of a digital Euro, as discussed in Chapter 2, these developments signal a paradigm shift. This is not just about modernising payment systems; it is about the potential for governments to exercise unprecedented control over individual finances. As outlined in Chapter 3, the risk of government surveillance, loss of personal privacy, and the ability to restrict or manipulate how money is spent are stark realities we must confront.

The digital nature of CBDCs introduces vulnerabilities that extend far beyond financial surveillance. Chapter 4 exposes the chilling prospect of cyber hacking and infrastructure attacks. In a fully digitised monetary system, the stakes are far higher than in traditional banking structures. A successful cyber attack on a CBDC could cripple an entire economy, unleashing financial chaos on a scale we have never witnessed before. The global interconnectedness of these systems makes them highly susceptible to cybercriminals, who could exploit weaknesses and trigger economic devastation.

However, the potential dangers of a cashless society are not confined to the realm of hacking or government overreach. In Chapter

6, we delve into the broader socio-economic consequences of a digital currency crash. Imagine a world where essential goods food, water, and fuel are inaccessible because citizens cannot access their funds due to a system failure or hack. The possibility of social unrest, political instability, and even revolution becomes all too real when people's very livelihoods are jeopardised. As history has shown, the breakdown of financial systems can quickly escalate into widespread social chaos.

The legal and ethical dimensions of CBDCs, as explored in Chapter 7, are equally troubling. With CBDCs, we face a future where financial systems could become tools of oppression. The potential for government control over individual spending, the erosion of civil liberties, and violations of basic human rights are not merely theoretical concerns. They are pressing ethical dilemmas that demand immediate attention. As governments around the world design legal frameworks for CBDCs, they must ensure that these laws respect personal freedoms and prevent the exploitation of digital currencies for authoritarian purposes.

On the global stage, CBDCs have already become entangled in the geopolitical power struggle, as described in Chapter 8. Nations like China, the US, and the EU are using CBDCs as instruments of influence, further complicating international relations. The ease with which financial sanctions could be imposed and enforced via CBDCs introduces a new layer of control that could reshape global trade, intensify conflicts, and destabilise already fragile alliances. Cross-border payments, once the domain of private financial networks, may soon become battlegrounds for international control and competition.

Nevertheless, it is essential to recognise that a cashless future is not without potential benefits. In Chapter 9, I explore the possibility of designing resilient CBDC systems that guard against hacking, technical failures, and government overreach. Decentralised blockchain technologies could offer a safer alternative or complement to centralised CBDCs, providing a layer of protection against abuse of power. Furthermore, the preservation of physical cash as a backup perhaps in a hybrid system could serve as a safeguard against the inherent risks of a fully digital monetary system.

The public must also play a role in shaping this future. Transparency, public debate, and citizen involvement are critical in ensuring that digital currencies are not thrust upon society without a thorough examination of their consequences. Open discourse is our best defence against the risks of hasty or ill-conceived implementations, and it is our responsibility as citizens to demand transparency and accountability from our governments.

As I reflect on the topics covered in this book, I am struck by the profound implications that CBDCs hold for the future of money, governance, and society. Are CBDCs an inevitable evolution of money, or are they a dangerous path towards totalitarian control? The answer is not clear-cut. What is certain is that we must tread cautiously. The future of money in a digital world is not predetermined it will be shaped by the decisions we make today. With thoughtful safeguards, ethical frameworks, and rigorous debate, we can harness the benefits of digital currencies while mitigating their perils.

This book is not meant to serve as a manifesto against progress, but rather as a call to pause, reflect, and prepare. In a world where control and chaos are two sides of the same coin, it is our collective duty to ensure that we steer towards a future where digital currencies serve the common good without sacrificing our freedoms, privacy, or security.

This foreword sets the tone for a book that explores both the promises and the dangers of a cashless future. I hope it provides readers with a balanced perspective, prompting them to question, engage, and seek solutions that preserve the values we hold dear in an increasingly digital world.

Chapter 1: The Evolution of Money: From Coins to Digital Currency

Overview: The Historical Progression of Money

The story of money is as old as civilization itself, a narrative that intertwines with humanity's growth from rudimentary social structures to complex, global economies. From the earliest barter systems to the sophisticated digital payments of today, the concept of money has constantly evolved, driven by necessity, innovation, and societal progress.

In ancient times, barter served as the primary method of exchange. I imagine the challenges faced by those early traders attempting to find someone who not only wanted what they had but who also possessed what they needed in return. This method, though effective in small, local settings, was inefficient and impractical as societies grew in complexity. As trade expanded, particularly between distant regions, the need for a standard medium of exchange became evident.

The introduction of metal coins, dating back to around 600 BCE, represented a significant leap forward. Coins, whether made from gold, silver, or bronze, had intrinsic value due to the material from which they were crafted. They also provided a uniform method of exchange that could be recognized across different regions and cultures. Coins held more than just monetary value; they were symbols of power, often stamped with the images of rulers and deities, reinforcing authority and control.

Paper money emerged as a revolutionary development in the evolution of currency. Originating in China during the Tang Dynasty, around the 7th century, it soon spread across the world. Paper money represented a shift from intrinsic to representative value where a note could represent a claim on a physical asset, such as gold or silver. This shift allowed for greater flexibility in trade and commerce, especially as societies moved into the mercantile and industrial ages.

As the world transitioned into the modern era, technological advances facilitated further change. The introduction of credit and debit cards in the mid-20th century heralded the beginning of the cashless society we are increasingly familiar with today. These cards, which allowed individuals to make purchases without physical currency, marked the initial steps towards digital transactions. The late 20th and early 21st centuries saw the rise of online banking, mobile payments, and a global shift towards electronic money transfers.

Yet, as much as the form of money has evolved, so too has the philosophy behind it. The move from tangible to intangible forms of currency poses questions of trust, security, and control issues that have become increasingly pertinent as we edge towards a cashless future.

The Rise of Cryptocurrencies

The introduction of cryptocurrencies represents the latest chapter in this evolving narrative. It was in 2009 that Bitcoin, the first cryptocurrency, emerged. At first, the concept of a purely digital currency was met with scepticism. How could something without physical form or state backing hold value? However, Bitcoin's revolutionary nature lies not just in its digital format but in its underlying technology: the blockchain.

The blockchain is, at its core, a decentralised ledger that records all transactions across a network of computers. This decentralisation is key to understanding the appeal of cryptocurrencies. Traditional currencies, whether coins or digital fiat money, are controlled by central authorities like governments or central banks. Cryptocurrencies, on the other hand, are governed by code and mathematical algorithms. This decentralisation offers a form of security that no central authority can provide, and it creates a level of transparency that could, theoretically, reduce corruption and manipulation.

Bitcoin may have paved the way, but it was not alone for long. Cryptocurrencies such as Ethereum, Ripple, and Litecoin soon followed, each bringing unique features and innovations. Ethereum, for instance, introduced the concept of smart contracts self-executing contracts with the terms of the agreement written directly into code. These cryptocurrencies, though speculative and volatile, represent a new way of thinking about money one that challenges the traditional financial system.

What fascinates me most about the rise of cryptocurrencies is how they have not only changed the way we think about money but have also forced central banks and governments to re-evaluate their role in the monetary system. The influence of cryptocurrencies has reached beyond the borders of the crypto community and has triggered a global conversation on the future of money.

The Concept of Central Bank Digital Currency

In response to the rise of cryptocurrencies, central banks around the world have begun exploring the concept of Central Bank Digital Currency (CBDC). But what exactly is CBDC, and how does it differ from cryptocurrencies like Bitcoin?

CBDCs are digital currencies issued and regulated by a country's central bank. Unlike cryptocurrencies, which are decentralised and operate on blockchain technology, CBDCs are centralised, meaning they are controlled and backed by a nation's monetary authority. This backing by a central authority is one of the key differences between CBDCs and cryptocurrencies. While Bitcoin's value is determined by market demand and supply, a CBDC would be pegged to the value of the national currency it represents, similar to how fiat currency operates today.

The objectives of introducing CBDCs are varied and multifaceted. For one, they could provide a more efficient and secure means of payment, particularly in a world that is increasingly moving away from cash. Moreover, CBDCs could offer financial inclusion to the unbanked population, as digital currency can be accessed with little more than a smartphone and an internet connection. In contrast, cryptocurrencies are often seen as being beyond the reach of everyday consumers due to their complexity and speculative nature.

Additionally, CBDCs could strengthen central banks' control over monetary policy. By issuing digital currency, central banks would have a direct connection to consumers, bypassing commercial banks. This could give central banks more effective tools to implement monetary policy, adjust interest rates, and respond to economic crises. Moreover, CBDCs could enhance transparency and reduce illegal activities, such as money laundering, by providing a clear trail of digital transactions.

Central Banks' Growing Interest

Over the past decade, we have seen growing interest in CBDCs from central banks across the globe. China, with its Digital Yuan, is arguably at the forefront of this movement. The People's Bank of China (PBOC) has been actively developing and testing its digital currency, with trials conducted in various cities. The Digital Yuan aims to reduce the country's reliance on cash, provide greater financial control, and compete with the growing influence of cryptocurrencies.

The United States, though more cautious, has also shown increasing interest. The Federal Reserve has been exploring the potential benefits and risks of a digital dollar, although it has yet to commit to any formal development. Similarly, the European Central Bank (ECB) has been assessing the introduction of a digital Euro, citing the need for a robust and secure European payment system in an increasingly digital economy.

The Bank of England has been evaluating the possibility of introducing a digital pound, intending to ensure the UK's financial system remains competitive in the digital age. Other nations, such as Sweden with its e-Krona, and Canada, are also exploring the potential of CBDCs.

The Dark Side of CBDCs: Risks to Individual Rights and Freedom

While proponents of Central Bank Digital Currencies (CBDCs) often champion their potential benefits such as increased financial inclusion, enhanced security, and the modernisation of monetary systems it is essential to also consider the grave risks they pose, particularly to individual rights and freedoms. The promise of efficiency, transparency, and control is enticing, but there is a darker, more troubling aspect of CBDCs that must not be overlooked.

A central feature of any CBDC is the level of surveillance and control it grants to the issuing government or central authority. In a system where every financial transaction is digitised and tracked, the government would have access to a comprehensive, real-time view of every citizen's financial life. This is not just a matter of knowing how much one earns or spends, but knowing precisely how every cent is used down to the coffee you purchase, the donations you make, or the organisations you support.

The idea of such a system, if wielded responsibly, may seem benign. But the question is, what happens when it is not? The risks of abuse in a CBDC-based system are profound. A government could, theoretically, gain the power to prohibit an individual from engaging in commerce altogether. For example, with a few keystrokes, an authority could freeze or delete the digital assets of anyone deemed a threat, dissenter, or member of a disfavoured group. The scale of this power is alarming such a mechanism could potentially erase the financial existence of an individual with unprecedented ease and efficiency. No government, no matter how well-intentioned, should have this kind of unchallenged control over its citizens' economic lives.

One needs only to look at real-world examples to appreciate the gravity of these concerns. In 2022, Chinese citizens who dared to criticise Chinese Communist Party General Secretary Xi Jinping by sharing photos of a protest banner saw their WeChat accounts abruptly suspended. WeChat, a ubiquitous "do-everything" app in China, is not only used for messaging but also as a primary method of payment. By losing access to WeChat, these individuals were not just silenced they were effectively cut off from society, and unable to pay for necessities like groceries, taxis, or public transport. This incident demonstrates the danger of a centralised digital system: a government, with minimal friction, can impose devastating consequences on individuals who dare to challenge the status quo.

Moreover, these concerns are not confined to authoritarian regimes. In 2022, the Canadian government used emergency powers to freeze the bank accounts of individuals participating in protests that the government deemed unlawful. This move, made under a system far less centralised and efficient than a CBDC would be, highlights the chilling potential for abuse in even democratic societies. The point here is not to argue the merits or demerits of these particular actions, but to underscore the potential dangers when governments wield financial control over their citizens. In a CBDC-based system, such powers would become even more accessible, faster to implement, and harder to challenge.

These examples should serve as stark warnings. The centralisation of financial control in the hands of a government, with the brutal efficiency of a CBDC, creates an environment ripe for overreach and abuse. It forces us to confront uncomfortable questions about who holds power in a society and how much of that power should be concentrated in a single entity. While today's financial system may be imperfect, its decentralised nature offers a level of protection from total government control. The ability to withdraw cash, use alternative payment platforms, or even rely on cryptocurrencies provides a form of financial autonomy that could be threatened by the implementation of CBDCs.

One of the critical arguments in favour of CBDCs is that they can deliver many of the core benefits proponents highlight, such as efficiency, inclusion, and security, but we must also recognise that these advantages can be realised through alternatives that do not grant unchecked power to any one authority. Blockchain technology, for example, has shown promise in enhancing security and transparency in a decentralised way, without necessarily placing full control in the hands of a central authority. Similarly, financial inclusion can be achieved through improved access to digital banking and financial services, without the need to abolish cash or implement a fully centralised digital currency.

In essence, a balance must be struck. The desire for modernisation and efficiency should not come at the cost of civil liberties and personal freedoms. The potential for CBDCs to provide governments with unparalleled control over the financial lives of individuals represents a risk that cannot be taken lightly. No government should possess the ability to monitor, control, or erase an individual's financial existence with a few keystrokes. The very nature of a digital currency must include safeguards mechanisms that protect citizens from the overreach of authority, ensuring that no government has the unchecked power to decide who can or cannot participate in the economy.

As the world grapples with the future of money, the introduction of CBDCs represents a pivotal moment. The risks, particularly to individual freedoms and the balance of power, must be weighed carefully. If we move forward without addressing these concerns, we may find ourselves in a world where financial control is centralised to a degree that threatens the very foundations of democracy and individual autonomy.

Thus, while the evolution of money continues, we must ensure that the digital future we build preserves the core values of freedom, privacy, and financial independence. In the rush towards modernisation, we cannot afford to lose sight of the fundamental principles that protect us from the excesses of power. The promise of CBDCs must be tempered by a commitment to these principles, lest we create a future where financial control becomes synonymous with political and social control.

In conclusion, we find ourselves at the crossroads of control and chaos. The shift towards digital currency, while inevitable, brings with it a host of new challenges. Cryptocurrencies have demonstrated the potential of decentralised finance, but they have also shown us the risks of volatility and speculation. On the other hand, CBDCs offer the possibility of a more secure and regulated digital currency, but they also raise concerns about surveillance, privacy, and the concentration of financial power.

As we move further into this new era, the evolution of money is far from over. The decisions we make now, as governments, institutions, and individuals, will shape the future of money and, by extension, the future of society itself.

Chapter 2: Global Trends in CBDC Implementation

As I reflect on the remarkable evolution of money, which I discussed in the previous chapter, it is clear that the rise of Central Bank Digital Currencies (CBDCs) is no longer a theoretical possibility but an impending reality. However, what strikes me most about this transformation is that, as with many such shifts in history, ordinary citizens have had little choice in the matter. We are hurtling towards a future where digital currencies, designed and implemented by central authorities, will reshape our financial systems and personal freedoms whether we ask for it or not. This is truly a brave new world that few of us voted for.

Each nation is carving its path toward this digital future, motivated by a mix of geopolitical ambition, economic strategy, and technological pressure. In this chapter, I will explore the diverse approaches to CBDC implementation across the globe, with a focus on China's Digital Yuan, the United States' cautious steps towards a digital dollar, the European Union's deliberations over a digital Euro, and the efforts of other nations such as Sweden, India, and Russia. The story that unfolds is one of power, control, and rapid change yet ordinary citizens largely left to adapt to a system they had little say in shaping.

China's Digital Yuan: A Geopolitical Power Play

China has been at the forefront of CBDC implementation, driving forward with the Digital Yuan (e-CNY) at an aggressive pace. Unlike the hesitant steps taken by other nations, China has already rolled out extensive trials, with its citizens in several cities now using the Digital Yuan for everything from public transport to online shopping. There is no opt-out here. The state has decided, and the people follow suit.

But what does this mean for the global order? The Digital Yuan is not just about efficiency or convenience; it is part of China's broader geopolitical strategy. By promoting a state-controlled currency that operates independently of Western financial systems like SWIFT, China is positioning itself as a financial power that can bypass US-dominated institutions. This is particularly crucial in a world where economic sanctions and trade restrictions often come hand-in-hand with geopolitical tensions. With the Digital Yuan, China can consolidate its economic influence, especially through initiatives like the Belt and Road, potentially reshaping global finance in its favour.

Yet, while the geopolitical implications are staggering, the impact on Chinese citizens is equally profound. The state already exerts significant control over personal freedoms, and the Digital Yuan could further tighten this grip. The currency's programmability allows for unprecedented surveillance over transactions, raising concerns about privacy and individual autonomy. For the average Chinese citizen, this is a new reality a currency that not only tracks their financial activity but can also potentially be programmed to control it. And, as ever, this brave new world was not something they had the luxury of voting on.

The United States and the Federal Reserve: Hesitant Steps Toward a Digital Dollar

In contrast to China's headlong rush, the United States has taken a far more cautious approach. The Federal Reserve has been researching the potential for a digital dollar for some time, but there has been no rush to implementation. Perhaps this reflects the scale of the potential upheaval such a move would bring to the American financial system. Banks, for instance, would face a major challenge. If citizens could hold digital dollars directly with the central bank, what role would there be for commercial banks, which currently rely on deposits to provide loans and sustain the economy?

Yet, despite these concerns, there is a growing sense that a digital dollar may be inevitable. In part, this is because the US must respond to the global competition created by China's Digital Yuan. A CBDC could reinforce the dollar's position as the world's reserve currency.

It could also improve financial inclusion for millions of unbanked Americans, offering them direct access to the formal economy without the need for traditional banking infrastructure. But let us not be naive. While the potential benefits of a digital dollar are often highlighted, there is little discussion about whether the American people want this. Most citizens are passive observers in this debate, with the decision-making power firmly in the hands of technocrats and policymakers.

Should the US proceed with a digital dollar, it will represent a monumental shift in the relationship between the state, the economy, and the individual. And yet, as we watch this debate unfold, we must remember that this, too, is a brave new world where most of us will have little say in the outcome.

The European Union and the Digital Euro: Unity or Fragmentation?

The European Central Bank (ECB) has been actively researching the potential of a digital Euro, yet, much like the United States, it remains in the exploratory phase. The challenge for the EU is particularly complex, given the multi-state structure of the Eurozone. How does one create a digital currency that works across 27 different countries with their financial regulations and priorities? The stakes are high on one hand, a digital Euro could enhance financial integration, making cross-border transactions more efficient and strengthening the union. On the other hand, it could exacerbate existing tensions, particularly between wealthier northern nations and those in the south.

For European citizens, the introduction of a digital Euro will likely be framed as a necessary step towards modernisation and efficiency. But again, the question remains: who asked for this? Much like the euro itself, the digital Euro will be a top-down initiative, with citizens expected to fall in line once the decision is made. While there are legitimate concerns about financial stability and the role of commercial banks, it is doubtful that the average European will have much influence over how or whether a digital Euro is introduced. The future of the European economy is being decided in Brussels and Frankfurt, not at the ballot box.

Other Countries: Experimentation and Exploration

While China, the US, and the EU dominate the global conversation on CBDCs, other nations are also making notable progress. Sweden, for example, has been pioneering the development of its e-Krona, driven by the rapid decline of cash usage in the country. Sweden's transition to a largely cashless society offers a preview of what the future may look like for many other nations. Yet, as with other CBDC initiatives, Swedish citizens have not been given a choice in the matter. As cash fades from daily life, the e-Krona becomes the de facto replacement, and with it comes the state's control over digital transactions.

India and Russia are also exploring CBDCs with their motivations. India, with its vast population and burgeoning digital infrastructure, sees potential in a digital rupee to modernise its economy. Yet, for a country with significant gaps in financial inclusion and digital literacy, one wonders whether the government is fully considering the broader societal implications of this shift. As for Russia, the development of the Digital Ruble is inextricably tied to its geopolitical situation, particularly as it seeks to insulate its economy from Western sanctions. But again, for ordinary Russians, this is another top-down change they have little control over.

Why Are Central Banks Developing Their Digital Currencies?

As we examine the rise of Central Bank Digital Currencies (CBDCs), it's important to understand why central banks are taking this route in the first place. The key drivers for CBDC development vary significantly between developed and emerging economies, revealing a complex tapestry of motivations that reflect the distinct economic realities of different regions. Developed nations, such as those in Europe and North America, are primarily concerned with maintaining their monetary sovereignty and enhancing the efficiency of payment systems. Meanwhile, in many emerging markets, financial inclusion is a critical motivating factor, as CBDCs are seen as a tool to bring millions of unbanked individuals into the formal economy.

For central banks in developed nations, the main goal is to future-proof their monetary systems. In an increasingly digital and globalised world, there is a fear that without state-backed digital currencies, these economies could lose control over their monetary policies and payment infrastructures. The rise of private digital currencies, such as stablecoins or even decentralised cryptocurrencies like Bitcoin, threatens to undermine the traditional role of central banks. By developing CBDCs, these nations hope to preserve their monetary sovereignty while ensuring that the state retains its role as the primary issuer of currency. Additionally, there is a desire to improve payment efficiency. Traditional payment methods especially for cross-border transactions can be slow, costly, and inefficient. A CBDC promises to streamline these processes, potentially lowering costs and making transactions faster and more transparent.

In contrast, for many emerging economies, the focus is on financial inclusion. In regions where a significant portion of the population remains unbanked or underbanked, CBDCs offer a direct way for individuals to participate in the financial system. In countries like Nigeria and the Bahamas, where physical banking infrastructure is sparse, digital currencies can provide a means of accessing financial services without relying on traditional banks. This motivation differs from developed countries, where banking infrastructure is already mature, and financial inclusion is not as pressing an issue.

Interestingly, central banks from outside Europe have observed more use cases for CBDCs than their Western counterparts. The main "live" CBDCs as of 2024 are not in the West but in countries like China, Nigeria, the Bahamas, and Jamaica. These nations are on the frontlines of digital currency adoption, providing a valuable testing ground for how CBDCs might function in real-world settings. However, it is worth noting that despite the early implementation of these digital currencies, their penetration remains relatively low. One key reason for this is that CBDCs have not yet been fully integrated with other payment systems or existing financial processes. As a result, uptake has been slow, and the transition from traditional to digital currency has been less seamless than anticipated.

A Long-Term Trend

The timeline for CBDC adoption and development is anything but short. Most CBDC projects will not be fully operational by 2024 or even 2025. Europe's digital Euro, for instance, is not expected to launch until sometime between 2026 and 2029. This reflects the cautious approach taken by many Western central banks, which are weighing the long-term economic and social implications of a digital currency before moving forward with full-scale implementation. The United States, for example, only published its first review of a potential CBDC in 2022, putting it significantly behind other nations that have already begun rolling out retail-focused digital currencies.

In developed countries such as Canada and the United Kingdom, much of the focus has been on how blockchain technology might optimise existing banking processes, rather than creating a consumer-facing CBDC. This approach contrasts sharply with nations like China and Nigeria, where retail CBDCs have been prioritised. One reason for this discrepancy may be concerns about privacy among citizens in Western nations. In the European Union, for example, there has been considerable public debate about the implications of a digital Euro, particularly regarding data privacy and surveillance. Many citizens are wary of a centralised digital currency that could potentially allow governments to track their every transaction, which has led to some resistance against the concept.

Yet, despite these concerns, CBDCs continue to attract significant attention, largely due to their potential to revolutionise day-to-day payments. The idea of a state-backed digital currency that is secure, efficient, and widely accepted appeals to both governments and businesses. Moreover, CBDCs stand in stark contrast to the decentralised design principles of cryptocurrencies. While Bitcoin, Ethereum, and other digital assets were created to circumvent centralised authority and empower individuals, CBDCs represent the exact opposite currencies that place the state firmly at the centre of the financial system.

Blockchain Technology and the Future of Money

One of the most significant aspects of CBDC development is its reliance on blockchain technology. This is particularly noteworthy because blockchain, up until now, has been primarily associated with cryptocurrencies like Bitcoin. For years, blockchain enthusiasts have argued that the technology has the potential to transform industries ranging from finance to supply chain management. Yet, CBDCs represent the first major use case where blockchain could be implemented on a wide scale, impacting billions of people globally.

But, unlike cryptocurrencies, which were designed to be decentralised, anonymous, and resistant to government control, CBDCs will likely embody the opposite characteristics. They will be centralised, trackable, and subject to government oversight. This sharp contrast between CBDCs and cryptocurrencies has fuelled much debate about the future of money and whether digital currencies will empower individuals or tighten state control over financial systems.

A Brave New Digital Frontier

As central banks continue to develop their digital currencies, it is clear that we are on the cusp of a fundamental shift in using money. However, this shift is being driven by forces beyond the control of ordinary citizens. Whether the motivation is to preserve monetary sovereignty, improve payment efficiency, or promote financial inclusion, the reality remains that the people most affected by these changes average citizens are often passive participants in this grand experiment.

The timeline for full-scale CBDC adoption is long, and many of the projects currently in development will not reach completion for several years. By then, the world's financial landscape will likely look very different from today. Whether CBDCs become the dominant form of currency, or merely one option among many, remains to be seen. But what is certain is that central banks will continue to play a central role in shaping the future of money whether we like it or not.

This brave new world of digital currencies is coming, and like so many technological revolutions before it, it is a world that few of us have voted for. The next chapter will explore the technical infrastructure required for CBDCs, examining the trade-offs between privacy, control, and efficiency as we navigate this unfolding digital frontier.

Conclusion: A Brave New World, But Not by Choice

The rise of CBDCs represents a turning point in the history of money, as governments and central banks reshape the financial systems that underpin our lives. But as we look around the world, one thing is clear: this is a future that citizens have not been asked to choose. Instead, it is being ushered in by policymakers, technocrats, and political elites, driven by a mixture of economic strategy and geopolitical rivalry.

Whether CBDCs will ultimately improve financial systems or create new forms of control remains to be seen. What is certain, however, is that the average citizen will have little say in the matter. As I discussed in Chapter 1, money has evolved through the ages from barter to coins, paper, and now to digital forms, but each transition has come with its trade-offs. This latest shift promises both opportunity and peril and as we navigate this brave new world, we must remain aware that it is one we did not vote for.

Chapter 3: Government Control and Surveillance through CBDCs

As I delve into this chapter, it's essential to build upon the foundation established in earlier sections of the book. In Chapter 1, we explored the evolution of money, from tangible coins and paper notes to the emergence of cryptocurrencies. By Chapter 2, we delved into the global trends in Central Bank Digital Currency (CBDC) implementation, with China, the US, the EU, and other nations leading the charge in developing state-backed digital currencies. Now, we shift our focus to the darker possibilities and the chilling consequences that such technologies may introduce.

Total Financial Control: The All-Seeing Eye of CBDCs

At the heart of government control through CBDCs lies the unparalleled potential for complete financial visibility. In a world where every transaction is digitally recorded and monitored, the anonymity that cash once provided vanishes. The government would gain the capacity to track every single purchase or transfer made by its citizens, creating a system of total oversight.

Such visibility would allow governments to intervene in ways previously impossible. Theoretically, they could freeze funds with a mere keystroke or dictate how money is used, overriding personal choice. This level of control could fundamentally reshape the relationship between individuals and the state. With the power to influence where money flows, governments could enforce policies with a terrifying level of precision. Imagine a society where dissenting voices could be silenced through financial strangulation, where economic freedom is no longer a matter of individual agency but a privilege granted or revoked by central authorities.

In Chapter 2, I highlighted China's Digital Yuan, a prime example of how state power can be intertwined with financial technology. The

Chinese government's surveillance infrastructure already extends into various aspects of citizens' lives, including social credit systems. The coupling of such systems with a CBDC framework could yield a form of control unparalleled in modern history. One must ask: how long before other nations, inspired by China's model, follow suit?

Loss of Anonymity: The Disappearance of Cash and Erosion of Privacy

In the age of cash, the flow of money allowed for a certain degree of anonymity. Whether in a bustling market or a private transaction between individuals, the exchange of physical currency provided a sense of privacy that has now come under threat. With CBDCs, the concept of untraceable transactions may become a relic of the past. Every financial movement would be logged in a centralised ledger, monitored in real-time, and retrievable at will by government authorities.

Loss of anonymity would not merely mean a forfeiture of privacy for those who are engaged in illicit activities. Everyday citizens, engaging in perfectly legal transactions, may suddenly find their every economic interaction subject to scrutiny. The government would have the capacity to track how much you spend, where you spend it, and potentially even why you spend it.

This also raises questions about the ethical implications of such surveillance. Could a government use this data to nudge citizens toward certain behaviours? Would spending on certain 'unapproved' items perhaps deemed unhealthy, immoral, or undesirable trigger penalties or restrictions? The digital age is already eroding privacy through social media, smart devices, and the internet. Adding CBDCs into the equation deepens the potential for an intrusive surveillance state, the likes of which Orwellian fiction once warned us about.

Programmable Money: The Perils of Smart Contracts

One of the defining features of CBDCs is their programmability. Unlike traditional currency, which can be spent freely without restriction, CBDCs can be engineered to include 'smart contracts' automated scripts that could govern how and when the money is spent. While the benefits of this technology are often touted in terms of preventing fraud, controlling subsidies, and promoting economic stability, significant dangers are lurking beneath these seemingly benign goals.

Imagine a world where your money can only be spent on government-approved goods and services. A CBDC embedded with smart contracts could theoretically restrict your ability to purchase certain items, travel to certain destinations, or donate to certain causes. Should a government decide that particular activities or ideologies are undesirable, it could program the currency to block any spending related to those sectors.

Moreover, governments could freeze accounts entirely, effectively cutting individuals off from economic participation. In a society where digital money is the sole means of transaction, the freezing of one's account would equate to an immediate loss of agency. This could be wielded as a tool of control, to suppress dissent or to enforce compliance with political or social mandates.

China's implementation of the Digital Yuan and its accompanying surveillance capabilities again provides a case study. While these technologies have been presented as measures to combat crime and bolster economic growth, they also carry the shadow of control. Could the same technology be deployed elsewhere? Chapter 2's analysis of the European Union's digital Euro shows a similar push towards a programmable financial future, though it remains to be seen how far such controls could extend.

Impacts on Personal Freedom: The Economic Handcuffs

At the core of this discussion is the question of personal freedom. What happens when financial independence the ability to choose how, where, and when we spend our money is taken away? The potential for governments to manipulate CBDCs goes beyond simple transactional oversight. It opens the door to an economic ecosystem where personal freedoms are fundamentally constrained by central authority.

In a world governed by CBDCs, citizens could find themselves living under constant economic surveillance, their every move tracked, and their financial autonomy limited. A system of programmable money, when controlled by the government, could be used to suppress opposition, direct behaviour, or maintain social order. Those who fall out of favour with the state could be economically ostracised, without the means to challenge the system or to live independently of it.

As I discussed in earlier chapters, the rise of cryptocurrencies offered the promise of decentralisation and the empowerment of individuals to take control of their financial lives. Yet, CBDCs represent the opposite a return to centralised control but with far more invasive tools at the government's disposal. In such a scenario, the question of "Who controls the money?" becomes synonymous with "Who controls the people?"

Governments, armed with the data of every transaction, could create a system where financial freedom is a luxury, not a right. This would have profound implications not just for economic independence but for civil liberties as well. The spectre of a cashless society governed by CBDCs could lead to an unprecedented level of state control over individual lives.

As we move forward in this book, we shall continue to explore the various perils and pitfalls of a cashless future. While CBDCs may bring certain efficiencies, their potential to infringe upon personal freedoms and grant governments unparalleled control cannot be ignored. The next chapters will delve deeper into the social and economic consequences of this shift, further exploring how such technologies may shape the world to come.

Three Key Prescriptions for a Balanced CBDC Future

As we've already seen, the potential for government control and surveillance through Central Bank Digital Currencies (CBDCs) is vast and concerning. The ability of governments to monitor every transaction, limit spending, and even freeze accounts introduces an unprecedented threat to personal freedoms. However, I believe that the introduction of CBDCs does not have to result in such dystopian outcomes. Indeed, there are ways to mitigate these risks, and I offer three key prescriptions that must be considered as CBDCs move closer to global implementation.

First, CBDC must not weaken the personal financial privacy available with today's paper cash.

One of the most cherished aspects of paper money is its ability to allow individuals to engage in transactions anonymously. From small daily purchases to more significant transfers of value, cash enables personal freedom by safeguarding financial privacy. If CBDCs are to be introduced, they must uphold this critical feature of financial autonomy.

CBDCs should incorporate privacy protections that ensure citizens can engage in lawful activities without their every transaction being recorded and scrutinised. Just as physical cash allows for private, untraceable exchanges, CBDCs must be designed to provide digital anonymity for legitimate transactions, preserving the rights and freedoms people currently enjoy. Privacy technologies such as cryptographic protections and decentralised architectures could help ensure that personal financial data is not indiscriminately accessible to governments or third parties.

Second, CBDC must not become a new, easier avenue for government agencies to surveil citizens, censor lawful activities, levy fines, and enact punishments.

The risk of overreach is a very real concern with CBDCs. Government surveillance, as we have discussed, could escalate to new levels of intrusion if the appropriate safeguards are not put in place. CBDCs must not be allowed to become tools for widespread government surveillance. Citizens should be free to engage in lawful activities without fearing that every financial move is being monitored or judged.

Governments may argue that enhanced surveillance can help prevent crime and enforce regulations more effectively, but this does not justify carte blanche access to every transaction made by every citizen. There must be limits on the state's ability to use CBDCs as a mechanism for punishment or censorship. Subpoenas, due process, and judicial oversight are all essential to ensure that governments do not abuse their access to financial data. Without these protections, CBDCs could become a dangerous tool for infringing upon civil liberties.

Third, the advent of CBDCs offers the opportunity to reassess contemporary financial surveillance activities in their entirety and rebalance them in better accord with democratic norms, the presumption of innocence, and the rule of law.

The introduction of CBDCs could provide a pivotal moment to reform the financial surveillance landscape that already exists. The sad truth is that, even before the advent of digital currency, our financial system was already subject to an extraordinary degree of government oversight. Financial service providers often compile detailed dossiers on their customers, share information among themselves, and report significant amounts of transactional data to governments without judicial oversight. This situation has become so normalised that many are unaware of the extent to which financial privacy has already eroded.

This prescription acknowledges the uncomfortable reality that financial surveillance is already pervasive, and the emergence of CBDCs could either exacerbate this problem or offer an opportunity to scale it back. Instead of accepting the status quo, we should seize this moment to challenge and reframe the role of financial surveillance. By developing a framework for CBDCs that respects individual privacy and adheres to the rule of law, we can push back against the overreach that has already taken root in our financial systems.

The Private Sector is No Better Protector of Privacy

Many argue that the development of digital money should be left to private-sector "stablecoin" developers, citing concerns that governments will inevitably use CBDCs for surveillance and control. However, it's critical to recognise that the private sector does not necessarily provide a haven for privacy either. Private financial institutions often engage in extensive surveillance practices themselves, as dictated by government regulations and market pressures.

Stablecoin developers and other non-sovereign digital currencies may face the same coercion from governments to monitor transactions, report suspicious activities, and comply with political pressures. Just as social media platforms have been subject to political influence censoring or promoting content based on prevailing ideologies private digital currency providers could easily fall prey to the same dynamics. In such an environment, financial privacy could be equally at risk, with private companies bowing to government demands just as public institutions do.

In democratic societies, lawful transactions whether made with CBDCs or private digital currencies must remain free from political surveillance and censorship. The protections we seek for financial privacy should extend across both public and private sectors, ensuring that neither is allowed to infringe on citizens' rights under the guise of protecting security or enforcing political correctness.

Ready or Not, CBDCs Are Coming

Whether or not the US and other democratic nations decide to fully embrace CBDCs, the global trend is undeniable. According to the Atlantic Council, 114 countries, representing over 95% of the global gross domestic product, are currently exploring or deploying CBDCs. Major economic players like India, Russia, Japan, and the European Union are moving swiftly toward implementing their versions of digital currency, and the pace of development shows no signs of slowing down.

In some of the freest societies on earth, including Sweden, Japan, and the UK, central banks are seriously considering the benefits and risks of CBDCs. The European Central Bank is expected to release a prototype for a digital euro by 2023, with wider deployment expected by 2025. These nations, often viewed as protectors of individual liberty, are spearheading efforts to bring CBDCs into the mainstream.

This digital gold rush is happening, whether the United States participates or not. Yet, the question remains: will CBDCs become surveillance coins tools of oppression, control, and censorship or will they evolve into freedom coins that respect privacy, personal autonomy, and civil liberties? If democratic nations like the US fail to act, they may leave the field wide open for authoritarian regimes to dominate the future of digital currency. The opportunity to shape CBDCs following democratic values must not be squandered.

Conclusion: A Crossroads for Financial Privacy

In conclusion, the future of CBDCs presents both enormous risks and significant opportunities. The current financial system is already deeply flawed when it comes to privacy, and CBDCs could exacerbate these problems or offer a chance to reset the balance. By ensuring that CBDCs protect personal privacy, limiting the scope of government surveillance, and reassessing the current state of financial oversight, we can chart a path forward that protects individual freedoms.

As CBDCs become an inevitable reality, it is up to us to determine whether they will evolve as instruments of control or as the digital embodiment of financial freedom.

Chapter 4: The Risk of Cyber Hacking and Infrastructure Attacks

As we advance further into the digital age, the move towards a cashless society driven by Central Bank Digital Currencies (CBDCs) brings with it a new wave of opportunities but also a significant set of vulnerabilities. Much of the excitement around CBDCs stems from their potential to revolutionise how we interact with money, simplifying transactions and enhancing the efficiency of financial systems globally. Yet, there is a darker side to this narrative one that exposes us to unprecedented threats to economic stability, security, and individual privacy. In this chapter, I will explore how the very infrastructure on which CBDCs are built could become the Achilles' heel of national economies. The threat of cyber hacking and infrastructure attacks presents a real and present danger, one that we cannot afford to ignore.

Vulnerability of Digital Networks

At the heart of any CBDC system lies a digital network, and it is this reliance on technology that creates its most glaring vulnerability. CBDCs, by their very nature, require an intricate web of digital communication platforms to function seamlessly. Unlike traditional fiat money, which can still circulate even when technological systems falter, CBDCs are intrinsically tied to these networks. Every transaction, every transfer of value, is logged and processed electronically. If this system were to be compromised, the consequences would ripple far beyond inconveniences at the checkout line or delayed transactions.

The more dependent we become on digital infrastructure, the more attractive a target it becomes for cybercriminals and even state-sponsored attackers. Consider the vast scale of cyberattacks we have witnessed in the past few decades, ranging from data breaches in multinational corporations to ransomware attacks crippling healthcare systems. The consequences of such attacks are magnified when applied to a national financial system, where the target is not merely a private organisation but the very lifeblood of a country's economy.

In Chapter 1, I discussed the evolution of money from physical coins to digital currency. In this evolution, physical cash served as a backup in times of crisis think of how people revert to cash during natural disasters or power outages. In a world where cash is obsolete, and CBDCs dominate, what happens when the digital infrastructure faces a massive cyberattack? The complete reliance on technology means that an attack on the network could bring national economies to their knees, leaving no alternatives for basic commerce or emergency transactions.

Cyber Attacks on CBDCs

The potential for sophisticated cyberattacks on CBDCs is one of the gravest concerns as governments move towards digitised monetary systems. In 2016, the Bangladesh Bank heist highlighted how vulnerable the global financial system could be to hacking. Cybercriminals exploited weaknesses in the SWIFT payment system, successfully stealing over $80 million. The breach sent shockwaves through the financial world, serving as a stark reminder that no system is impervious to attack. If such a breach could occur in a well-established financial network like SWIFT, one can only imagine the damage that could be done to an entirely digital monetary system.

Cyberattacks on CBDCs could take many forms, from Distributed Denial of Service (DDoS) attacks designed to overload and crash systems to more insidious forms of malware that could manipulate or reroute transactions. Worse still, a coordinated attack on the digital infrastructure of CBDCs could result in mass data corruption, rendering large portions of the monetary system unusable.

Another fear is that hackers could steal CBDCs directly from central banks or financial institutions, shaking public confidence in the currency. In Chapter 3, I touched on the issue of government control and surveillance, but ironically, the same tools of oversight that governments could use to track transactions might also be hijacked by cybercriminals to achieve nefarious goals.

Ransomware Attacks

One of the most concerning forms of cybercrime in recent years has been ransomware attacks, where malicious software locks systems or data until a ransom is paid. We have seen this tactic used against private companies and public institutions, but what if cybercriminals set their sights on CBDCs? In a cashless world, ransomware could take on an entirely new level of severity.

Consider a scenario where a ransomware attack targets a central bank's CBDC system. The attackers could lock the entire digital monetary system, effectively freezing all transactions in a country until the ransom is paid. Such a scenario is not far-fetched; similar attacks have paralysed hospitals, factories, and municipal governments. The sheer scale of disruption that could result from a ransomware attack on a CBDC system is terrifying. No one would be able to access their funds, make payments, or even buy essentials like food and medicine. The ransom demanded would likely be astronomical, and governments may face a no-win situation pay the criminals and risk setting a dangerous precedent or refuse to pay and watch their economy grind to a halt.

Moreover, the structure of CBDCs could make it easier for ransomware attackers to target not just governments but also individuals. In the same way that personal bank accounts are hacked today, individual CBDC wallets could become the focus of ransomware schemes, with cybercriminals threatening to lock users out of their own money unless a payment is made. The vulnerabilities are manifold, and as I discussed in Chapter 2, governments around the world are racing to implement CBDCs, but not all seem fully prepared for these eventualities.

Governments' Preparation

How well-prepared are governments to handle the security risks associated with CBDCs? While there has been significant investment in cybersecurity by both governments and private institutions, the speed at which digital threats evolve often outpaces the solutions designed to counter them. In my view, many governments are still playing catch-up, particularly when it comes to understanding the full scope of the risks.

Governments must contend with a range of challenges. First, there is the issue of securing the core infrastructure of CBDCs protecting central banks, digital wallets, and the networks that facilitate transactions. Then, there's the question of international cooperation. Cyberattacks do not respect borders, and a weak link in the global financial system could become a gateway for cybercriminals to attack multiple countries at once.

Regrettably, many governments have been reactive rather than proactive in their approach to cybersecurity. While nations like China have invested heavily in securing their digital yuan, other countries seem less prepared. The European Union, for example, is still grappling with the complexities of implementing a digital euro, while the United States, despite its technological might, has not yet fully addressed the scale of cybersecurity threats posed by a digital dollar.

As I touched upon in Chapter 2, global trends in CBDC implementation are uneven. Countries are rushing to be first movers in this space, but in doing so, they may be underestimating the risks. A fully digitised monetary system is only as strong as its weakest link, and the consequences of an attack on this system could be catastrophic. We are entering uncharted territory, where the speed of technological advancement may outpace the security measures needed to protect it.

The Escalating Cost of Cybercrime and Emerging Threats for 2024

As we've discussed earlier in this chapter, the digital landscape supporting Central Bank Digital Currencies (CBDCs) is fraught with vulnerabilities that expose national economies to significant risks. According to a 2023 report from **Cybersecurity Ventures**, the global cost of cybercrime reached a staggering $8 trillion, and it is expected to rise to **$10.5 trillion** by 2025. This translates to more than $250,000 per second a financial bleed that no sector, especially digital financial infrastructures like CBDCs, can afford to ignore. These figures underscore the relentless growth of cybercrime, and with them in mind, it's crucial to examine the most pressing cybersecurity threats for 2024 and explore strategies to mitigate them.

As we continue into 2024, the cyber threats that plague digital networks are evolving in both complexity and frequency. In this section, I will outline the key cybersecurity threats that could specifically target CBDC infrastructures and discuss strategies that governments and institutions must adopt to safeguard against these emerging dangers.

Types of Cybersecurity Threats

Cyber threats to CBDC systems can be categorised into several types, each posing a unique set of challenges. From malware and ransomware to social engineering and insider threats, these dangers highlight the multifaceted nature of modern cybercrime. Let us delve into the primary threat vectors that are most concerning in the context of a fully digital monetary system.

Malware Threats

Malware continues to be one of the most prevalent and damaging forms of cyberattacks, and its evolution poses an ever-present threat to CBDC systems. Malware encompasses a wide range of malicious software, including viruses, worms, ransomware, spyware, and more. In a digital financial environment, malware can cripple operations, compromise sensitive data, and corrupt the entire network.

- **Viruses and Worms:** Traditional yet effective, viruses and worms continue to wreak havoc by spreading through digital ecosystems, often exploiting vulnerabilities in network systems. Worms, in particular, are self-replicating and can spread without human intervention, making them especially dangerous for a CBDC infrastructure that relies on interconnectivity between financial institutions, businesses, and consumers.

- **Ransomware:** As noted earlier, ransomware attacks have surged dramatically. According to the **World Economic Forum**, ransomware activity increased by 50% in the first half of 2023, and this trend has continued into 2024. The rise of **Ransomware as a Service (RaaS)** has lowered the barrier to entry for cybercriminals, allowing even those with minimal technical expertise to launch attacks. For a CBDC system, a ransomware attack could mean the paralysis of national economies until exorbitant ransoms are paid. Given that many ransomware demands are made in cryptocurrencies to preserve anonymity, this threat is particularly insidious.

- **Cryptojacking:** Another form of malware is **cryptojacking**, where cybercriminals hijack computer systems to mine cryptocurrency without the user's knowledge. While not as directly disruptive as ransomware, cryptojacking can severely drain a system's resources, compromising the performance of essential services that CBDC networks depend on.

- **Fileless Malware:** One of the more advanced threats for 2024 is **fileless malware**, which executes malicious code directly from a system's memory rather than through traditional files. This makes it exceedingly difficult to detect and mitigate using conventional antivirus software, putting even the most secure digital financial systems at risk.

To combat these malware threats, institutions must adopt a **layered cybersecurity approach**. This includes regular software updates, **comprehensive end-user education** to prevent phishing attacks, advanced threat detection systems, and rigorous access controls. As discussed earlier in this chapter, employing a robust cybersecurity framework is essential, and regular audits are critical for the early detection and mitigation of these threats.

Social Engineering Attacks

Social engineering is one of the most insidious types of cybercrime because it preys on human psychology rather than technological vulnerabilities. It is particularly concerning for CBDC systems, where attackers can manipulate individuals to gain access to critical financial infrastructure.

- **Phishing Variants:** Phishing attacks have evolved in 2024, with **spear phishing**, **vishing** (voice phishing), and **smishing** (SMS phishing) becoming increasingly sophisticated. For example, spear phishing targets individuals with highly personalised messages, often crafted to appear as legitimate correspondence from colleagues or institutions, manipulating employees into divulging sensitive information.

- **Baiting and Pretexting:** These methods exploit human curiosity and trust. For instance, baiting schemes may involve distributing USB drives purportedly containing essential work-related data but instead loaded with malware designed to infiltrate corporate or government networks. **Pretexting**, where attackers pose as legitimate authorities to request confidential information, has also seen increased use, especially in environments where employees are less vigilant due to remote working or busy schedules.

Given the human factor in these attacks, **education and awareness campaigns** within organisations are crucial. Employees must be trained to recognise social engineering tactics and multi-factor authentication should be implemented as a standard measure to prevent unauthorised access to CBDC-related systems.

Insider Threats

One of the more alarming categories of cyber threats is the **insider threat**, which arises when individuals within an organisation either intentionally or accidentally compromise security. These threats are particularly concerning in the context of CBDCs, as they bypass many external security measures.

- **Accidental Threats:** Sometimes, employees unknowingly open a backdoor for attackers, for instance, by clicking on a phishing email or using weak passwords. These lapses can be mitigated through regular cybersecurity training and the enforcement of stringent security protocols.
- **Malicious Insiders:** More worryingly, malicious insiders can exploit their legitimate access to cause intentional harm, such as leaking sensitive information or sabotaging systems. In a CBDC system, such actions could have catastrophic consequences, from manipulating financial records to aiding external attacks.

To defend against insider threats, organisations should implement **zero-trust security architectures**, which ensure that no one inside the network is inherently trusted. Continuous monitoring and segmentation of networks are also vital, allowing early detection of unusual activity.

Advanced Persistent Threats (APTs) and Supply Chain Attacks

Advanced Persistent Threats (APTs) are highly sophisticated and stealthy attacks, often carried out by state-sponsored actors. These attacks aim to infiltrate networks and remain undetected for long periods, gathering intelligence or slowly destabilising systems.

- APTs targeting CBDCs would likely seek to undermine confidence in the digital currency by corrupting data or subtly interfering with monetary policies. Given their sophistication, these threats are incredibly difficult to detect and defend against.

Similarly, **supply chain attacks** exploit the trust we place in third-party vendors. By compromising software or hardware components before they even reach consumers, attackers can introduce vulnerabilities into systems that are otherwise thought to be secure. In a CBDC context, a supply chain attack could potentially compromise the entire infrastructure before it is even operational.

Distributed Denial of Service (DDoS) Attacks and MitM Attacks

Lastly, **DDoS attacks** and **Man-in-the-Middle (MitM) attacks** continue to pose severe threats in 2024. While DDoS attacks aim to overwhelm systems with traffic, disrupting services, MitM attacks intercept and manipulate communications between parties, potentially compromising transactions or stealing sensitive information. For CBDCs, which rely on continuous and secure operations, such attacks could have a devastating impact on public trust and economic stability.

Defence Strategies for 2024 and Beyond

Given the increasing scale and complexity of cyber threats in 2024, it is evident that defending CBDC systems will require more than just reactive measures. Governments and institutions must embrace a **proactive cybersecurity strategy** that combines cutting-edge technology with robust organisational policies.

Key strategies include:

1. **Adopting a Zero-Trust Security Model:** Assume that

threats can come from anywhere, both inside and outside the organisation.

2. **Implementing AI-Driven Threat Detection:** Use advanced algorithms and machine learning to detect and respond to threats in real-time.

3. **Regular Audits and Stress Testing:** Conduct routine security assessments and simulate potential attacks to identify vulnerabilities before they can be exploited.

4. **End-User Education:** Continuous training programmes for employees to recognise and respond to social engineering and phishing attempts.

5. **International Cooperation:** As cybercrime knows no borders, global coordination is essential for tracking and mitigating large-scale attacks.

By implementing these strategies, we can begin to address the cyber threats shaping the financial landscape in 2024, safeguarding CBDCs and the broader digital economy from the perils of a cashless future.

Conclusion

The risk of cyber hacking and infrastructure attacks is one of the most pressing challenges in the transition towards a cashless society. CBDCs hold tremendous potential, but they also open the door to a new era of cybercrime one in which the stakes are higher than ever before. As we march towards a future where cash no longer exists, the need for robust, resilient cybersecurity measures becomes paramount. Failure to address these risks could lead us into a world where our financial systems are not controlled by central banks or governments, but by those with the technical prowess to exploit their weaknesses.

Chapter 5: The Perils of Technological Dependency

As we move towards an increasingly digitised monetary system, one cannot ignore the perils of technological dependency, especially in the context of Central Bank Digital Currencies (CBDCs). The convenience of instant payments and the efficiency of cashless transactions are undeniable, but so too are the risks inherent in relying so heavily on technology for the backbone of an entire financial system. In this chapter, I will explore some of the most pressing concerns that arise from this dependency, ranging from electromagnetic pulse (EMP) threats to systemic failures and technical glitches. The digital future promises efficiency, but as I shall argue, it is also fraught with significant vulnerabilities.

Electromagnetic Pulse (EMP) Threats

One of the more catastrophic risks posed by our reliance on digital infrastructure is the threat of an electromagnetic pulse (EMP) attack. Whether it comes from a natural event like a solar flare or as a result of human action, such as terrorism, an EMP has the potential to bring down entire power grids, rendering digital banking systems useless.

Solar flares, also known as coronal mass ejections (CMEs), have historically caused disruptions to the Earth's magnetic field. A notable incident occurred in 1859, known as the Carrington Event, where a solar storm knocked out telegraph systems across continents. If a similar event were to occur today, it would undoubtedly cause far more severe damage, given our reliance on electricity for every facet of life, particularly our financial systems. The consequences would be devastating. The backbone of a CBDC is its digital network, and an EMP could quite literally fry the circuitry that keeps this infrastructure operational. Without access to physical money as a backup, we would be thrust into chaos, with people unable to access their funds to purchase essential goods or services.

The risk of a man-made EMP attack, potentially deployed by a rogue state or terrorist group, adds another layer of concern. If hostile actors were to target the digital banking infrastructure, the effects could be equally catastrophic. One EMP could bring the entire banking system to a grinding halt, not just locally but potentially on a global scale. Chapter 4 explored the risks of cyber hacking and infrastructure attacks, but EMP threats transcend even the most sophisticated digital defences, cutting directly to the physical infrastructure that powers the financial world.

Systemic Banking Failures

The prospect of a nationwide or even global digital banking failure is not far-fetched in a world where all money is funnelled through a single, centralised system. I have touched upon this in earlier chapters, particularly in discussing the risks of governmental overreach and surveillance (Chapter 3), but here we confront an even more existential threat: the collapse of the very system that underpins our economy.

In a fully cashless world, where digital currency reigns supreme, the implications of systemic failure would be dire. Without the safety net of physical currency, citizens would find themselves unable to access money for vital needs food, medicine, and shelter. Panic would quickly set in as shops would struggle to accept payments, and the very fabric of society could begin to unravel. We have already seen glimpses of this during periods of financial instability or technological failure. Consider the public's response during outages of major online banking platforms: queues at ATMs, people stockpiling cash, and widespread frustration. Now imagine that scenario on a much larger scale, with no cash fallback whatsoever.

The risks are amplified in the context of international trade, where CBDCs could become the norm for cross-border payments (as outlined in Chapter 8, 'Geopolitical Ramifications'). A failure in one nation's CBDC system could have far-reaching consequences, disrupting global markets and supply chains. In a world connected by digital threads, the collapse of one strand could quickly lead to the unravelling of many others.

Technical Glitches

Even in the absence of catastrophic events like EMPs or systemic banking failures, everyday technical glitches pose a significant threat to the stability of a cashless society. Server outages, software bugs, or simple human errors could disrupt the ability to transact digitally, leaving individuals and businesses unable to make payments.

We've seen such glitches occur in the existing financial system, where even small outages can lead to widespread disruption. A temporary server failure at a bank may prevent people from accessing their accounts or making payments, but in a world reliant on CBDCs, the stakes would be much higher. If the centralised infrastructure supporting CBDCs were to experience a technical glitch, it could leave entire populations unable to transact, with no access to physical cash as a backup.

While some may argue that these issues are solvable through robust design and redundancy, the truth is that no system is infallible. Even with the most rigorous safeguards in place, the complexity of digital currency networks means that technical failures are inevitable. The real question is how prepared we are to deal with such disruptions. Governments and central banks may assure us that contingency plans are in place, but as with many aspects of technological dependency, the potential for unforeseen consequences remains.

The Risk of Losing Power

The digital infrastructure that powers CBDCs is, of course, entirely dependent on electricity. What happens when the lights go out? In the event of a power outage whether caused by natural disasters, grid failures, or targeted attacks entire regions could be cut off from the financial system.

Without access to electricity, citizens would find themselves unable to charge devices, access the internet, or make digital payments. In such a scenario, a cashless society would come to a standstill. Basic transactions would become impossible, and those without access to alternative sources of energy would be particularly vulnerable.

In Chapter 6, I will delve further into the social implications of such failures, particularly the unrest that could arise when people are unable to meet their basic needs. But for now, it is important to recognise that power outages are not a rare occurrence. Natural disasters such as hurricanes, earthquakes, or floods frequently knock out power for extended periods, and while most of us take for granted the resilience of the grid, its fragility is well documented.

Moreover, in an era of increasing geopolitical tension, the risk of targeted attacks on critical infrastructure cannot be dismissed. Chapter 8 will explore how CBDCs could become a tool of geopolitical warfare, but here we must acknowledge that energy grids themselves are a target. A concerted attack on a nation's power grid could be just as effective as an EMP in crippling its financial system.

The perils of technological dependency are vast and varied, with each scenario posing a significant risk to the stability and security of a cashless society. From EMP threats and systemic banking failures to everyday technical glitches and the fragility of our power grids, the potential for disruption is ever-present. As we march towards a digital future, we must be acutely aware of these risks and take steps to mitigate them.

Earlier chapters have outlined the promise of CBDCs, but with that promise comes the need for resilience. As I will explore in subsequent chapters, particularly in Chapter 7 ('Legal and Ethical Implications') and Chapter 9 ('Safeguards and Alternatives'), building redundancy into the system whether through maintaining cash as a backup or ensuring robust regulatory oversight will be critical to navigating the challenges that lie ahead.

The Perils of Technological Dependency

In addition to the various threats already discussed, the complete dependency of CBDCs on electrical power introduces one of the most alarming risks to a fully cashless society. As digital transactions become the sole means of financial exchange, the reliance on electricity becomes absolute. Without it, the entire system could collapse, bringing day-to-day commerce to a halt. This dependency magnifies the dangers of power outages, whether caused by natural disasters, grid failures, or targeted attacks such as EMP strikes.

As I briefly mentioned earlier, without electricity, citizens would find themselves unable to charge their devices, access the internet, or make digital payments. In a world where physical money no longer exists, this would have catastrophic consequences. However, we must dig deeper into the broader implications of such a scenario, which extends beyond mere inconvenience to the very foundation of societal order.

The Collapse of Supply Chains and the Onset of Anarchy

Our modern economic system is built on just-in-time delivery models, particularly in sectors like food and retail. This means that businesses keep minimal stock on hand, relying instead on continuous, timely deliveries to meet consumer demand. In a cashless society, the digital infrastructure would play a critical role in keeping these supply chains functional. Payments between suppliers, distributors, and retailers would flow seamlessly through digital channels until, of course, the lights go out.

In the event of an EMP strike or a prolonged power outage, food shortages would almost immediately arise. Without the ability to process payments, trucks would cease to move, warehouses would sit idle, and grocery stores would be unable to restock. The fragility of our supply chain, already strained during events like natural disasters or pandemics, would snap entirely. Within days, panic would set in as people realised they could not access the necessities of life.

If an EMP attack were to occur, the situation would worsen exponentially. Not only would digital payments be rendered useless, but most modern transportation systems would also fail. An EMP could permanently damage the electrical systems in vehicles, effectively immobilising the logistics network that supplies the entire country. In such a scenario, we would lose not just the means to transact, but the means to transport goods altogether.

It is worth noting that the consequences of such a breakdown would extend far beyond food. Medicine, fuel, and essential supplies would be in similarly short supply, heightening the risk of social unrest. People would likely turn to whatever alternatives they could find to survive, and in this grim landscape, traditional barter systems would re-emerge. Guns, ammunition, and tangible assets such as silver and gold would become the currency of choice, as they retain value independent of the digital networks now rendered useless.

With no functioning financial system, no law enforcement capable of maintaining order, and no government able to provide immediate relief, anarchy would prevail. This chilling prospect leads to the unavoidable question: **Have governments fully considered the social consequences of their push for digital control?**

A Blind Spot in Government Preparedness?

Governments and central banks are undoubtedly aware of the technical and security challenges involved in the adoption of CBDCs. As outlined in Chapter 4, cyber hacking, ransomware, and other forms of digital attack have been considered and, in theory, planned for. But have these institutions adequately prepared for the more fundamental risks posed by electrical grid failures or EMP threats? Have they fully grasped the cascading effects that a prolonged loss of electricity would have on a cashless society?

While nations have begun to harden their critical infrastructure against cyberattacks, little evidence suggests that similar efforts are being made to address the broader vulnerabilities of a power-dependent financial system. The potential for large-scale social breakdown in the absence of electricity is rarely, if ever, discussed in public forums about CBDCs. There is an unsettling sense that in the pursuit of efficiency and control, governments may be underestimating the fragility of the system they are building.

If CBDCs are to become the cornerstone of our future financial architecture, then contingency planning must extend beyond cybersecurity and digital redundancy. It must account for the very real possibility of electrical grid failures, whether from natural disasters, EMPs, or other catastrophic events. Moreover, it must address the societal implications of such failures: the collapse of supply chains, the reversion to barter economies, and the risk of widespread anarchy.

Conclusion

As we continue to embrace the digital future, we must not allow ourselves to be blinded by the promise of convenience and control. The perils of technological dependency are not abstract, and the scenarios I have discussed EMP threats, systemic banking failures, technical glitches, and power outages are more than theoretical. They are real, tangible risks that demand our attention.

Governments and central banks must take these risks seriously, and the public deserves to know whether adequate safeguards are in place. As I will explore in Chapter 9, 'Safeguards and Alternatives,' building resilience into the CBDC system whether through decentralised solutions, maintaining cash as a fallback, or ensuring robust oversight is not just a matter of prudence. It is essential for safeguarding the future of our society in a world where technology and infrastructure are inextricably linked.

If we are to avoid the chaos that could arise from these perils, we must prepare not only for the digital risks but also for the very real possibility that the lights might go out and with them, the entire financial system as we know it.

In a world where control and chaos are in constant tension, we must tread carefully, lest we find ourselves at the mercy of the very technology we sought to master.

Chapter 6: Economic Disruption and Social Unrest

In a cashless future where Central Bank Digital Currencies (CBDCs) dominate the financial landscape, the possibilities for economic disruption are vast. While the promise of CBDCs lies in efficiency and convenience, the risks loom large, especially in the case of systemic failures. As I have discussed in earlier chapters, especially in Chapter 4 on cyber hacking and infrastructure vulnerabilities, a major failure of a CBDC system could have catastrophic consequences, not just for individual users but for entire economies. In this chapter, I will explore the immediate economic effects of a major CBDC failure, how the inability to purchase essentials could lead to social chaos, and the broader political consequences of such an event.

Immediate Economic Effects

Imagine a world where one morning the CBDC system fails perhaps due to a cyberattack or infrastructure collapse, as outlined in the earlier chapter on cyber vulnerabilities. The ramifications would be immediate and severe. In financial markets, panic would ensue. Investors would scramble to pull out their assets, fearing the worst. If the system fails at the level of a major currency, like the digital dollar or digital yuan, global markets would likely react with sharp declines, uncertainty, and chaos.

The effect on currency valuation could be devastating. With no physical cash alternative, citizens would find themselves locked out of the financial system. Currency devaluation could follow as confidence in the system erodes. In extreme cases, this could even lead to hyperinflation as the value of the CBDC plummets and governments attempt to introduce more digital currency to stabilise the system.

Historically, when faith in the monetary system is shattered, chaos often follows. The Weimar Republic's hyperinflation in the 1920s serves as a potent reminder of how quickly things can spiral out of control. A failed CBDC could provoke similar conditions in modern economies, only at a much faster and more widespread scale due to the instant and interconnected nature of digital currencies.

Inability to Purchase Essentials

A far more personal impact of a CBDC collapse would be the sudden inability of ordinary people to purchase essential goods like food, water, and fuel. Digital wallets would be rendered useless. Supermarkets, petrol stations, and utility providers reliant on the CBDC for transactions would be unable to process payments. This raises the very real spectre of a society where citizens find themselves unable to access even the most necessities.

We have already seen in real-world scenarios how banking failures can lead to social chaos. One such example is the collapse of the banking system in Greece in 2015 when capital controls were imposed, and citizens were limited in how much they could withdraw from ATMs. Panic ensued, with long queues forming outside banks and people scrambling to stockpile cash, food, and medicines. Now imagine such a scenario, but with no cash alternative available at all only digital wallets that are effectively frozen.

In the event of a widespread CBDC failure, it wouldn't just be a question of banks restricting withdrawals; the entire economy could seize up. Those reliant on digital payments would be stranded. This could happen on a national or even global scale, depending on the architecture of the CBDC system. Whether it's the elderly relying on digital pensions, workers receiving their salaries digitally, or consumers using digital payments for everyday transactions, the consequences would be widespread and immediate.

Social Unrest and Political Consequences

As history has shown, when people are unable to meet their basic needs, social unrest quickly follows. If millions are unable to buy food, water, or fuel, the conditions are ripe for widespread protests, riots, and even revolution. In a fully digitised economy, this risk is magnified exponentially.

Consider the events of the Arab Spring, where food shortages, economic instability, and political repression led to uprisings across the Middle East and North Africa. Now imagine similar tensions, but driven not by political repression but by a sudden inability to access money and meet basic needs due to a digital currency failure. What might begin as localised unrest could quickly spiral into a national or even global movement, as citizens worldwide find themselves locked out of the financial system.

The political consequences would be enormous. Governments may attempt to regain control through martial law, curfews, or even internet shutdowns, further exacerbating the situation. It is easy to foresee a scenario in which citizens lose trust not only in their financial system but in their governments as well. The result could be a breakdown in the social contract, where citizens no longer believe that the state is capable of providing for their needs or ensuring their economic security.

Moreover, a CBDC crash could lead to the rise of alternative economies, whether through bartering or the resurgence of black-market cash economies. As I explored in Chapter 3 on government control through CBDCs, such a scenario could severely undermine state power, as citizens seek ways to circumvent a broken system. Ironically, the very control that governments sought to achieve through CBDCs could be undone by the backlash that follows a failure.

Global Financial Panic: The Cascading Effects of a Major CBDC Failure

In a world where CBDCs form the backbone of global finance, the failure of a single major CBDC such as the digital dollar or digital yuan would send shockwaves through the entire financial system. As outlined in Chapter 4, these digital currencies are intrinsically tied to national economies and, by extension, global markets. A failure due to a cyberattack or infrastructure collapse would not be an isolated incident confined to one country; it would likely have a cascading effect across borders, markets, and industries.

The most immediate reaction would be a wave of panic across financial markets. Investors, driven by fear and uncertainty, would rush to liquidate their assets, attempting to salvage whatever value they could before the situation worsened. Stock markets, already highly sensitive to economic signals, would likely experience severe drops as institutional investors and private traders alike scramble to exit positions. Such a massive sell-off would, in turn, erode confidence even further, creating a self-reinforcing loop of panic and capital flight.

For emerging economies and nations with weaker currencies, the fallout could be even more catastrophic. These countries often rely heavily on foreign investments and international trade, both of which are highly dependent on the stability of global financial systems. If a major CBDC like the digital dollar or yuan collapses, it could trigger a massive withdrawal of foreign capital from these markets, leading to currency crises, debt defaults, and possibly even economic collapse. The interconnected nature of the global economy means that even countries with relatively stable financial systems could find themselves engulfed in the resulting chaos.

The commodities market would also be severely impacted. Essential goods such as oil, natural gas, and agricultural products are often priced in major global currencies, like the US dollar. A sudden devaluation or freezing of digital dollars due to a CBDC collapse would create uncertainty in the pricing and trading of these commodities. Supply chains could seize up as companies struggle to make payments, leading to shortages and price spikes. The instability would only compound the difficulty for ordinary citizens, who, as previously discussed, would already be facing the inability to purchase essential goods due to the collapse of the CBDC system.

Moreover, a CBDC failure could lead to a resurgence of national protectionism and economic isolationism. Countries, desperate to shield their economies from the fallout, might impose trade barriers, capital controls, or even sever digital payment links with other nations. The global financial system, which has been built on principles of interdependence and open markets, could fragment into isolated blocs, further deepening the economic disruption and delaying any potential recovery.

Finally, the impact on central banks themselves would be profound. Central banks have long been viewed as the guarantors of financial stability. A failure of a CBDC the very digital currency issued by these institutions would severely undermine their credibility. Trust, once lost, is difficult to regain, and the inability of central banks to manage or mitigate the effects of a digital currency collapse could lead to a crisis of confidence in centralised financial authorities as a whole. This loss of trust could further fuel the rise of decentralised cryptocurrencies or alternative monetary systems, which might appeal to citizens and investors seeking to regain control over their financial destinies outside the traditional banking infrastructure.

In essence, the collapse of a major CBDC would have far-reaching consequences that extend beyond national borders. Financial markets would plummet, emerging economies could crumble, and global trade would grind to a halt. The world would be plunged into economic uncertainty, with trust in central banks and traditional financial systems eroded, potentially pushing global economies towards fragmentation and alternative forms of currency and trade.

This scenario underlines the fragility of an over-reliance on digital currencies without the safeguards and redundancies of a robust financial infrastructure. While CBDCs promise efficiency and modernisation, they also carry the risk of massive disruption, should their underlying systems fail. In a world where every transaction, every trade, and every investment is dependent on the flawless functioning of digital networks, the potential for catastrophic failure cannot be ignored.

In conclusion, while a cashless future promises efficiency and convenience, it also brings with it new risks that could destabilise economies and societies. A major failure of a CBDC system would likely lead to immediate economic disruption, social unrest, and far-reaching political consequences. As we have seen in earlier chapters, the vulnerability of digital networks, the risk of cyberattacks, and the potential for government overreach all contribute to the fragility of a cashless future. This chapter serves as a warning: the perils of a fully digitised economy are real, and the consequences of failure could be devastating.

If we are to move toward such a future, we must do so with our eyes wide open, fully aware of the risks and prepared for the potential fallout. The stakes could not be higher.

Chapter 7: Legal and Ethical Implications

In this chapter, I delve into the legal and ethical ramifications of Central Bank Digital Currencies (CBDCs), as they represent a seismic shift in how we think about money, governance, and personal freedoms. This discussion builds upon the themes explored in earlier chapters particularly those focused on government control (Chapter 3), cyber risks (Chapter 4), and economic disruption (Chapter 6) by examining the broader framework within which CBDCs will function. The potential for overreach, manipulation, and human rights violations requires us to ask serious questions about the legal and ethical boundaries that should govern these new financial systems.

Digital Currencies and Legal Frameworks

As governments worldwide explore the implementation of CBDCs, one question looms large: how will the legal frameworks be designed? Historically, legal frameworks around currency have evolved slowly, adapting to societal changes over decades or centuries. The transition from coins to paper money, and later to credit cards and electronic payments, was gradual. Yet, CBDCs represent a leap forward, not an evolution, and the legal structures we design must be robust enough to govern such a powerful tool from the outset.

Governments will need to strike a delicate balance. On the one hand, regulations must ensure the stability of financial markets, protect consumers, and prevent illegal activities like money laundering. On the other, these frameworks could easily morph into tools of mass surveillance and control if left unchecked. Will laws around CBDCs respect personal freedoms? Or will the new frameworks designed to govern digital currencies encroach upon civil liberties in the name of security and efficiency?

In Chapter 3, I discussed how the rise of programmable money might lead to unprecedented levels of government oversight. Imagine a scenario where legal frameworks permit the government to freeze accounts at will or limit how individuals spend their money. These controls could be presented as tools to fight crime, but in the wrong hands, they could be used to stifle dissent or suppress vulnerable communities.

Legal scholars must ask: What safeguards can be embedded into the legal system to prevent this kind of overreach? How will courts interpret cases of government intervention in private financial transactions? Existing legal frameworks often treat money as a private matter, but CBDCs could blur the line between the personal and the public, pushing us into an era where every transaction is subject to scrutiny.

The Ethics of Total Financial Control

Is it ethical for governments to wield total control over an individual's financial life? This question is at the heart of CBDC development. In earlier chapters, I explored the potential for governments to monitor and control every transaction a person makes (Chapter 3). From an ethical perspective, this kind of control is troubling.

The ethical implications of CBDCs are not confined to financial transparency. They extend into questions of autonomy, freedom, and the right to self-determination. It is one thing for a government to regulate large financial institutions and enforce tax compliance. It is another thing entirely to design a currency system that could allow for real-time tracking and manipulation of personal spending habits.

One might argue that CBDCs are not inherently unethical; after all, they are a tool, and their ethical value depends on how they are used. But the potential for misuse is staggering. We must ask whether the risks of creating such a powerful tool outweigh its benefits. The surveillance potential alone raises ethical red flags. Under what ethical framework should these systems be developed? Should citizens have a say in the design of CBDC governance?

Transparency, accountability, and consent should be guiding principles in the development of CBDCs. Without these ethical foundations, we risk entering a future where individuals are stripped of their economic agency under the guise of progress.

CBDCs and Human Rights

The introduction of CBDCs could lead to serious infringements on basic human rights. Three rights stand out as particularly vulnerable: the right to privacy, the right to free association, and the right to economic independence.

In Chapter 3, I touched on how the elimination of cash might result in the loss of anonymity in financial transactions. With a fully digital currency, every purchase, transfer, or donation could potentially be monitored by the government. The right to privacy is enshrined in numerous international treaties and constitutions, but CBDCs could make this right difficult, if not impossible, to protect. Financial privacy is often the first line of defence against oppressive governments. Whether it is activists receiving donations or everyday citizens buying sensitive items, the ability to act without fear of constant surveillance is a cornerstone of a free society.

Beyond privacy, CBDCs could also infringe on the right to free association. Financial systems are not neutral; they have the power to shape and control social relationships. If governments can track and restrict who sends money to whom, this could have a chilling effect on civil society. Non-profit organisations, religious groups, or political movements could find themselves under financial pressure if their transactions are scrutinised or restricted. Economic independence one's ability to earn, save, and spend money freely is foundational to many other rights. A CBDC system that limits or manipulates access to funds could effectively strip citizens of this independence.

Governments must ensure that any future CBDC respects human rights, and international bodies like the United Nations should play a key role in holding nations accountable.

Precedents in Financial Control and the Erosion of Free Association

While the risks of Central Bank Digital Currencies (CBDCs) to privacy and economic independence are critical to examine, we must recognise that many of these issues are not hypothetical. Even before the full-scale implementation of CBDCs, we are already witnessing instances where financial systems are being weaponised to shape social behaviour, restrict association, and exert political pressure. These precedents highlight the potential for similar abuses once CBDCs become a centralised and easily controlled instrument.

One particularly alarming example occurred in **Canada** during the **2022 "Freedom Convoy" protests**, where truck drivers opposed COVID-19 vaccine mandates and other governmental restrictions. The Canadian government invoked the **Emergencies Act**, which gave it sweeping powers to freeze the bank accounts of protestors and their supporters. While the government argued this was a necessary measure to prevent funding of what it saw as an unlawful protest, it demonstrated how easily access to one's financial resources can be curtailed in response to political actions. The decision to target not only the protestors but also individuals and organisations donating to the cause sent a chilling message: financial systems can be used to enforce political conformity. If such measures were enacted through a CBDC, where the state has immediate and centralised control over digital transactions, the potential for widespread abuse becomes even greater.

The Social Credit System in China and Parallels in Western Governments

In China, the **Social Credit System** (SCS) stands as a stark warning of how financial systems, when fused with state oversight, can infringe on civil liberties, including the right to free association. Although the Digital Yuan has not been formally integrated into this system, the SCS already functions as a mechanism of social control, with far-reaching implications. The system assigns scores to citizens based on their social and financial behaviour, with high scores resulting in rewards such as easier access to credit, housing, and employment while low scores lead to severe restrictions. These can range from denial of access to loans, exclusion from job opportunities, and even limitations on travel. The central premise of the SCS is that non-conformity to state-sanctioned norms is penalised through the denial of economic independence and social mobility.

The Chinese model offers a glimpse into a future where the integration of Central Bank Digital Currencies (CBDCs) could create an even more efficient tool for social control. In a CBDC regime, the state's ability to track every transaction could be weaponised to target those who oppose the political establishment. Imagine a world where attending a protest, donating to a political cause, or simply expressing dissent could result in an automatic reduction in your social credit score or even an immediate freeze on your digital funds. Such a system would make it nearly impossible for individuals to exercise their right to free association without fear of economic retribution.

While the Social Credit System may seem unique to China's authoritarian governance structure, we must consider how similar mechanisms are beginning to emerge in **Western democracies**, particularly under left-leaning governments that advocate for greater social and political oversight. In these contexts, financial systems are increasingly being used as tools to enforce ideological conformity, often under the guise of promoting "social justice" or preventing harm.

One notable example is the growing trend of **deplatforming** and **financial blacklisting** by major financial institutions and payment processors in the West. Companies such as **PayPal** and **GoFundMe** have made headlines for cancelling accounts or freezing funds associated with individuals and organisations whose political views run counter to mainstream progressive ideals. These actions, often taken in response to pressure from left-leaning governments, activist groups, or public opinion, demonstrate that financial services are already being leveraged to marginalise certain viewpoints. This is particularly concerning when we consider how easily these practices could be expanded under a CBDC system, where governments have direct control over the currency itself.

For instance, in the wake of politically charged events, such as the **2020 Black Lives Matter protests** or debates around **climate change**, left-leaning governments have shown a willingness to push for financial repercussions for those deemed to be on the "wrong side" of the ideological divide. In some cases, businesses and individuals who support causes that contradict government-approved narratives, such as conservative political movements or fossil fuel industries, have faced pressure from financial institutions to cease operations or divest. This echoes the core principles of China's Social Credit System, where loyalty to the state and adherence to social norms are rewarded, while dissent and deviation from accepted political values are punished.

Moreover, the increasing use of **ESG (Environmental, Social, and Governance)** scoring by financial institutions in the West parallels aspects of China's SCS. Under the ESG framework, companies and individuals are scored based on their environmental impact, social responsibility, and corporate governance. While this may seem innocuous on the surface, the reality is that these scores can determine access to credit, investment opportunities, and insurance. A company or individual with a low ESG score could find themselves financially disadvantaged, much like a Chinese citizen with a low social credit score. As left-leaning governments push for more stringent ESG regulations, there is a growing concern that these systems could be weaponised against those who hold contrarian views, especially in areas like climate policy or social justice.

In both China and the West, financial systems are increasingly being tied to behavioural expectations. In China's case, the expectations are explicitly tied to loyalty to the Communist Party, while in the West, they are often linked to progressive social values. Both systems, however, share a common thread: the use of economic levers to enforce political and social conformity. The potential for abuse in a CBDC system is enormous. Once governments have direct control over digital currencies, they could easily freeze accounts or limit spending based on a citizen's adherence to state-approved ideologies. The **programmability of CBDCs** would allow governments to restrict purchases, donations, or investments deemed "unacceptable," making it even easier to punish dissent without the need for overt legal action.

For example, left-leaning governments in the West could use a CBDC system to limit or even block donations to political movements or organisations that oppose their policies. Charitable donations to religious organisations that hold traditional views on marriage or gender, for instance, could be scrutinised, and transactions blocked under the justification of promoting social equality. Similarly, individuals or groups advocating for reduced government intervention in climate policy could find themselves financially marginalised if their transactions are restricted due to a low ESG or similar social score.

While these examples may seem speculative, the groundwork is already being laid. The increasing cooperation between governments and financial institutions in monitoring and regulating financial behaviour demonstrates how easily CBDCs could be employed for social control. Just as China's Social Credit System links every aspect of a citizen's life to their economic standing, so too could Western CBDC systems link an individual's political, social, and environmental behaviour to their access to financial resources.

In conclusion, the rise of CBDCs poses significant risks not just to privacy and economic independence, but to the very foundations of free association. While China's Social Credit System offers a dystopian vision of what could be, the policies and practices already emerging in the West indicate that this future may not be as distant or as foreign as we might hope. As we move towards a cashless society, the centralisation of financial control in the hands of governments, whether authoritarian or democratic, raises profound concerns about the potential for widespread suppression of dissent and ideological conformity. The lessons from both China and the West make it clear: unless strong legal and ethical safeguards are put in place, CBDCs could become the ultimate tool for state-sponsored social engineering.

A further example can be seen in the way **international sanctions** are implemented. While these sanctions are often used as a tool of geopolitical strategy, they illustrate the power of financial systems to control and punish associations between individuals, corporations, and even entire nations. **SWIFT**, the global messaging system for financial transactions, has frequently been used to sever countries such as **Iran** and **Russia** from the global financial system in response to their political actions. Although these measures are typically justified on the grounds of international security, they show how financial systems can be leveraged for political purposes. A CBDC would make it even easier for governments to impose sanctions on a smaller scale, targeting individual dissidents or groups within their borders with the same level of efficiency currently applied to nation-states.

Moreover, payment processing companies such as **PayPal**, **GoFundMe**, and others have occasionally restricted or cancelled accounts associated with controversial figures or organisations. These actions often occur at the behest of governments or in response to social and political pressures. While private companies operating within the current financial system might claim they are acting in line with their terms of service, the broader issue is clear: financial systems are already being used to control who can receive or send money. If this trend continues in a world where CBDCs dominate, the potential for widespread social control through financial means becomes far more likely.

These examples underscore a critical point: financial systems, even before the implementation of CBDCs, are not neutral actors. They possess the power to influence social and political relationships by either enabling or restricting financial transactions. The chilling effect this can have on civil society, non-profit organisations, and political movements cannot be overstated. When money flows are controlled, so too are the people and organisations that rely on that money to sustain their operations.

The transition to CBDCs threatens to take these precedents to an even more invasive level. Once governments control both the currency itself and the infrastructure that processes every transaction, the ability to restrict free association and curtail economic independence becomes dangerously efficient. The question, therefore, is not whether financial systems will continue to exert control over social relationships, but to what extent CBDCs will amplify this control and at what cost to civil liberties.

In the absence of sufficient legal and ethical safeguards, the centralisation of financial power in the hands of governments could stifle dissent, suppress non-conformity, and erode the fundamental freedoms that underpin democratic societies. The experiences in Canada, China, and the broader international financial system offer a sobering reminder that these dangers are not distant possibilities, but present realities.

Conclusion

As we move towards a future dominated by CBDCs, we must carefully consider the legal and ethical frameworks that will govern these currencies. The potential for government overreach is immense, and without strong legal safeguards, CBDCs could erode the very foundations of a democratic society. Ethical considerations must also be at the forefront of the debate, ensuring that digital currencies do not become tools of oppression or control.

The right to privacy, the freedom to associate, and economic independence are all at risk if CBDCs are implemented without sufficient oversight. In earlier chapters, I explored the economic and technological risks of a cashless society, but the legal and ethical implications are perhaps even more profound. The choices we make now will shape the future of personal freedoms in ways that will reverberate for generations. We must ensure that this future is built on the principles of justice, fairness, and human dignity.

Chapter 8: Geopolitical Ramifications

In previous chapters, we explored the technical, ethical, and socio-economic consequences of a cashless future. From the legal frameworks that underpin Central Bank Digital Currencies (CBDCs) to the heightened risks of cyberattacks, and the societal tensions that may arise from economic disruption, it is evident that CBDCs are not merely technological innovations they are political instruments. In this chapter, I delve into how the introduction of CBDCs is reshaping global power dynamics, and what this could mean for international relations, financial sanctions, and the future of global trade.

The Global Power Struggle: How CBDCs are Becoming Another Tool in Geopolitical Competition

The emergence of CBDCs has introduced a new front in the ongoing geopolitical competition between global powers. Just as military might, economic clout, and technological superiority have historically determined the global hierarchy, digital currencies now sit on the same pedestal. In Chapter 2, I detailed China's ambitious push with its Digital Yuan, an initiative that has not only allowed Beijing to leap ahead of many developed nations but has also provided a potent weapon in its geopolitical arsenal.

China's dominance in this space is unsettling for both the United States and the European Union. The US dollar has long been the de facto global currency, anchoring the world's financial system, while the Euro has maintained a strong regional hold. But with the rapid development of the Digital Yuan, China seems poised to challenge this dominance, especially in regions where it wields economic influence through initiatives like the Belt and Road. The ability to bypass traditional payment networks such as SWIFT, which has historically been controlled by the West, gives China an edge in forging alliances with nations wary of Western hegemony.

The US, meanwhile, has been slower in its approach, as discussed in Chapter 2, but the Federal Reserve's cautious exploration of a digital dollar reflects its recognition of the stakes involved. The European Union, similarly, has expressed concerns about the geopolitical implications of lagging, with the European Central Bank pushing forward with the concept of a digital Euro. These developments set the stage for an intricate power struggle, where nations wield CBDCs not just as monetary tools but as instruments of influence, pushing their digital currencies into the global market to win over trading partners, both willing and reluctant.

Financial Sanctions and CBDCs: A New Era of Economic Warfare?

In Chapter 3, we explored how CBDCs could grant governments unprecedented control over personal and commercial transactions. On a larger scale, this control has massive implications for international diplomacy, particularly when it comes to sanctions. Traditionally, sanctions have been a key mechanism for powerful nations to exert pressure on rogue states or individuals. The West, in particular, has used financial institutions and payment networks like SWIFT to enforce these measures, as seen in the sanctions against Iran and North Korea.

With the advent of CBDCs, sanctions could become even more pervasive and difficult to evade. CBDCs could allow governments to precisely target the flow of funds, freezing assets, or blocking transactions with a level of granularity that traditional banking systems simply cannot achieve. If the US or the EU were to implement such tools through their digital currencies, they could enforce financial isolation on a scale previously unimaginable. However, this increased ability to monitor and control international payments also raises the question: what happens when nations resist?

China's Digital Yuan could offer an alternative to the Western financial architecture, enabling sanctioned states to bypass US and EU-controlled networks. In this sense, CBDCs could not only sharpen the effectiveness of sanctions but also render them less potent when competing currencies are used as escape routes. This duality illustrates the complex chessboard of global finance, where CBDCs could either entrench Western financial dominance or erode it, depending on how the cards fall.

The Role of CBDCs in Global Trade: Streamlining or Creating Tensions?

One of the potential promises of CBDCs is the streamlining of global trade. In theory, digital currencies could make cross-border transactions more efficient, reducing the friction caused by exchange rates, intermediary banks, and outdated payment systems. Chapter 1 explored how the rise of digital transactions has already laid the groundwork for such a shift, and CBDCs seem like the logical next step.

Yet, this simplicity may come with hidden costs. Imagine a future where each global power insists on the primacy of its own CBDC in trade negotiations. The result could be a fragmented global trade landscape where businesses are forced to navigate competing digital currency ecosystems. For instance, a company trading with both the US and China might have to maintain liquidity in both the Digital Dollar and the Digital Yuan, subjecting itself to the political whims of both powers. This scenario could lead to heightened tensions between countries as they push for their CBDC to become the international standard, much like how the US dollar currently serves that role.

Furthermore, countries with weaker economies may find themselves pressured to adopt the CBDCs of more powerful nations, compromising their financial sovereignty. This dynamic risks deepening the global divide between developed and developing countries, as smaller nations become ever more dependent on the economic policies of CBDC-issuing powers.

Cross-Border Payments and International Control: Who Holds the Keys?

A key question that looms over the rise of CBDCs is: who controls the flow of money across borders? In the existing financial system, institutions like the International Monetary Fund (IMF), the World Bank, and the SWIFT network play critical roles in facilitating international payments. But CBDCs could upend these traditional structures, creating new power dynamics in cross-border trade.

As I discussed in Chapter 6, CBDCs bring with them the risk of financial instability, and this risk becomes even more acute in cross-border payments. The movement of digital currencies across nations could be subjected to strict regulatory controls, and the temptation for governments to impose capital controls limiting how much money can flow in or out of a country could be overwhelming in times of crisis. Such measures would not only destabilize global markets but could also cause diplomatic rifts between nations as they scramble to protect their economic interests.

Nations that dominate the CBDC landscape may gain disproportionate control over the global financial system. As it stands, the US and China appear to be the most likely candidates for such dominance, with the European Union and other regions trailing behind. How these powers choose to wield that control, and whether they do so in cooperation or competition, will shape the future of global trade and international relations.

The Western Response: A Hybrid Approach to CBDCs and the SWIFT Challenge

The rise of China's Digital Yuan, as detailed in earlier sections, has sent shockwaves through the Western financial establishment, particularly because it directly challenges the dominance of the US dollar and, by extension, Western control over global financial systems such as SWIFT. As China seeks to establish the Digital Yuan as a viable alternative to traditional payment networks, it poses a serious threat to one of the West's most powerful tools: the ability to enforce economic sanctions.

Historically, the SWIFT network has been a key mechanism for imposing financial sanctions, particularly by the United States and the European Union. SWIFT, a global messaging system used for international payments, is heavily regulated by Western governments, and any nation or individual excluded from this system finds it nearly impossible to conduct business on the world stage. This was exemplified in sanctions against Iran and North Korea, which saw them essentially cut off from the global financial system.

China's Digital Yuan represents a new challenge to this model. By allowing countries to bypass SWIFT altogether, the Digital Yuan could offer rogue states an alternative financial lifeline, rendering Western sanctions ineffective. Nations such as Russia, Iran, and Venezuela, which have long been the targets of economic sanctions, could find themselves turning to China's digital currency as a means of conducting trade and securing international transactions, free from the watchful eyes of Western powers.

The Western Response: Towards a Hybrid System

Faced with this threat, Western governments find themselves in a difficult position. On one hand, they must counter the geopolitical and financial influence that China wields through the Digital Yuan. On the other, they must avoid disrupting their economies or restricting the freedoms of their citizens in the process. The solution being explored by many in the West is a hybrid system, one that incorporates the advantages of CBDCs without abandoning the structures that have maintained Western financial dominance.

In the United States, the Federal Reserve is researching the potential for a Digital Dollar that would operate within a broader hybrid financial system, as mentioned in Chapter 2. The Digital Dollar would be designed not to replace the existing financial infrastructure but to coexist with it. This approach allows the US to maintain the supremacy of the dollar as the global reserve currency while offering an alternative digital currency for more efficient transactions. A hybrid system also ensures that the US remains central to international financial systems like SWIFT while exploring ways to modernise cross-border payments to compete with China's offering.

Europe is similarly cautious. The European Central Bank's (ECB) proposal for a Digital Euro, as explored in previous chapters, highlights a careful balancing act. The ECB acknowledges the necessity of digitising Europe's currency to keep up with global trends, yet it remains committed to preserving the Euro's position within the existing financial system. A hybrid system, where digital currency operates alongside traditional banking and payment mechanisms, allows European nations to strengthen their economic standing without threatening their financial infrastructure.

Containing the Threat: Mitigating the Sanction-Evading Capabilities of the Digital Yuan

Western governments are also developing strategies to mitigate the risk that China's Digital Yuan could become a tool for sanction evasion. One approach is the enhancement of international cooperation in regulating CBDCs. Governments could introduce global frameworks that require CBDCs to adhere to certain standards, ensuring that even digital currencies are subject to scrutiny under international law.

Moreover, Western nations are investing heavily in blockchain technology and distributed ledger systems. As discussed in earlier chapters, one of the most powerful features of CBDCs is the transparency they can provide in tracking the flow of money. By using advanced blockchain solutions, Western governments could develop their own secure, highly regulated digital currencies that still allow them to monitor transactions, even in a cashless, digital future.

Another crucial consideration is the development of more sophisticated sanction mechanisms, tailored specifically for a world where digital currencies dominate. Traditional sanctions, which rely heavily on banking and financial intermediaries, will need to evolve. In this new landscape, sanctions may involve freezing digital wallets, blocking transactions within CBDC networks, or using blockchain analytics to trace illicit funds. These tools would allow the West to continue imposing economic pressure on rogue states while adapting to the realities of digital financial systems.

Hybrid CBDCs: The Balance Between Control and Freedom

One of the key challenges facing Western governments is how to introduce CBDCs without infringing on the freedoms of their populations. As detailed in Chapter 3, the potential for CBDCs to facilitate government surveillance and financial control is a major concern. Western democracies must tread carefully to avoid creating systems that echo the more authoritarian uses of CBDCs, such as China's Digital Yuan, where the government has full oversight of all transactions.

A hybrid system offers a potential solution. By allowing CBDCs to exist alongside cash and traditional financial systems, Western nations could ensure that citizens retain the option to make anonymous purchases or conduct transactions without fear of government surveillance. This system could also offer greater financial resilience, as individuals would not be forced to rely solely on digital currencies, which are susceptible to cyberattacks, network failures, and other risks discussed in Chapter 4.

Governments could implement safeguards to ensure that CBDCs respect personal freedoms. For example, laws could be enacted to limit the government's ability to access transaction data without a warrant, thus protecting privacy. Moreover, CBDCs could be designed with optional anonymity features for smaller transactions, ensuring that individuals can still conduct their financial affairs without intrusive oversight.

The path forward will require careful diplomacy, cooperation, and innovation. As the world becomes increasingly digital, the balance between control and freedom, dominance and competition, will define the future of global power. The next frontier in this battle is already being waged not on the battlefield, but in the algorithms and networks that underpin the digital currencies of tomorrow.

Conclusion: Navigating the New Geopolitical Terrain

The geopolitical ramifications of CBDCs extend far beyond simple currency competition. The rise of China's Digital Yuan has introduced a significant challenge to the West's ability to enforce sanctions and maintain control over the global financial system. However, Western governments are not without options. By adopting hybrid CBDC systems that combine the strengths of digital currencies with the established financial order, they can maintain their geopolitical standing without sacrificing the freedoms of their populations.

These digital currencies are not merely tools for modernising financial systems but are potent instruments of power in a world already fraught with economic and political tensions. The competition between global powers to control the future of money could either streamline global trade or exacerbate existing rivalries. Financial sanctions may become more effective but also easier to evade with alternative CBDCs. And finally, the control over cross-border payments could shift the balance of power in ways that are difficult to predict but will undoubtedly have long-lasting consequences for the global order.

As we continue to explore the perils and pitfalls of a cashless future, it becomes ever clearer that CBDCs are not just about efficiency or convenience they are about control. And in the hands of global powers, that control will extend far beyond national borders, influencing international relations, trade, and the lives of individuals around the world.

Chapter 9: Safeguards and Alternatives

In a world that is rapidly moving towards digitalization, the concept of a Central Bank Digital Currency (CBDC) poses many questions that extend far beyond its immediate utility. The risks are manifold, as I have explored in earlier chapters, from **economic disruption** and **geopolitical ramifications** to the very real **threat of government control and surveillance**. But in this chapter, I aim to focus on the safeguards and alternatives we must consider to protect ourselves from the pitfalls of a cashless society. This is not a debate to be taken lightly, nor one that can be left solely to governments and central banks. The integrity of our financial system, and indeed, our freedoms, may well depend on the decisions made in the coming years.

Building Resilient Systems

When thinking about how governments might design CBDCs to be resilient, I must first acknowledge the glaring vulnerabilities of a purely digital monetary system, which I detailed in **Chapter 4** on cyber hacking and infrastructure attacks. CBDCs, by their nature, are reliant on a vast, interconnected digital infrastructure. This creates a central point of failure that could lead to catastrophic consequences in the event of a cyberattack or technical failure. To mitigate these risks, resilience must be built into the very core of any CBDC system.

Redundancy is a key concept here. Multiple fail-safes should be in place, such as the creation of backup systems that are not entirely digital. These backups could operate on parallel networks or even involve offline mechanisms to ensure that, in the case of a disruption, citizens can still access their funds and perform essential transactions. This harkens back to the discussions in **Chapter 6**, where I illustrated the chaos that could ensue if people were unable to buy food, water, or fuel due to a digital collapse.

But resilience goes beyond technical fixes. It must also involve a robust **governance structure**. A CBDC system should be designed with checks and balances to prevent the misuse of power. This leads us directly to the next important question: how do we guard against the centralization of too much control in too few hands?

The Role of Blockchain Technology

One potential solution that has been gaining traction is the integration of blockchain technology into the design of Central Bank Digital Currencies (CBDCs). In **Chapter 1**, I discussed how cryptocurrencies like Bitcoin, which operate on decentralized ledgers, have pioneered a way forward for digital currencies. While CBDCs are fundamentally different from cryptocurrencies, blockchain could offer an alternative approach that mitigates some of the risks associated with centralization.

A **decentralized ledger** as opposed to a fully centralized system managed exclusively by a central bank could provide an extra layer of security. The idea is that by decentralizing the control of the ledger, it becomes significantly harder for bad actors, whether they are hackers or authoritarian governments, to manipulate the system. In **Chapter 3**, I addressed the dangers of programmable money, where governments could restrict the way citizens spend their money or freeze accounts altogether. A decentralized ledger could act as a safeguard against this type of abuse by distributing control among a broader network.

However, it is important to recognize that blockchain technology also has its **limitations**, particularly when applied to CBDCs. One of the primary challenges lies in ensuring **scalability**. Cryptocurrencies like Bitcoin and Ethereum have already shown how difficult it can be to process a large volume of transactions on a decentralized network without experiencing delays or increasing costs. This challenge would be exponentially greater for a national or global CBDC system, where millions of transactions must be processed in real time. The **current technological limitations** of many blockchain systems make them impractical for large-scale adoption in their present form. However, ongoing innovations in **Layer 2 solutions** and other scaling technologies may address these bottlenecks, making a hybrid blockchain-based CBDC system more feasible in the future.

Another consideration is the balance between **privacy and transparency**. One of the advantages of blockchain technology is that it can offer a transparent, immutable ledger, where transactions are publicly verifiable. This could help to **increase trust** in the system, especially when it comes to the governance and oversight of a CBDC. In **Chapter** 7, I discussed the importance of regulatory checks and preventing the abuse of power, and blockchain could serve as a tool to ensure greater **accountability**. However, there is also the issue of **privacy**. A fully transparent blockchain, where all transactions are visible to everyone, would effectively eliminate financial privacy. For CBDCs, this would be unacceptable for most citizens, as it could lead to excessive surveillance and a loss of personal freedom.

One potential solution to this dilemma is the use of **permission blockchains**, where only authorized entities, such as regulatory bodies or financial institutions, have access to the full transaction history. Meanwhile, individual users could still retain a degree of privacy, with only necessary data being shared with the authorities in cases of legal scrutiny. This approach could help strike the delicate balance between **regulatory oversight** and the protection of **individual rights**, which I have argued is critical to the success of any CBDC system.

Furthermore, blockchain could facilitate the integration of **smart contracts** self-executing agreements with the terms of the contract directly written into code. While smart contracts hold immense potential for automating complex transactions and enhancing financial efficiency, they also pose new risks. As I mentioned in **Chapter 3**, the idea of programmable money could lead to governments or other authorities imposing restrictions on how individuals use their funds, such as limiting purchases or freezing accounts based on predefined criteria. If improperly implemented, smart contracts could be used to enforce **authoritarian controls** over personal spending. Thus, any use of blockchain technology in the design of CBDCs must carefully consider how to regulate and implement smart contracts without infringing on **personal freedoms**.

Lastly, there is the issue of **interoperability**. If various nations adopt CBDCs, particularly those built on different blockchain platforms, there could be significant challenges in facilitating **cross-border payments** and **international trade**. As I explored in **Chapter 8**, CBDCs will likely play a major role in reshaping the global financial landscape. However, for this to happen smoothly, we must ensure that different CBDC systems are compatible with one another. Blockchain technology, with its potential to standardize and simplify international payments, could help address these concerns. By using open-source or interoperable blockchain frameworks, CBDCs from different countries could interact seamlessly, reducing friction in global trade and **cross-border payments**.

In conclusion, blockchain technology offers a promising yet complex solution to many of the challenges associated with CBDCs. Its decentralized nature could provide an extra layer of security and act as a check against government overreach, while its potential for transparency could increase trust in the system. However, technological limitations, privacy concerns, and the risk of misuse through programmable money all present significant challenges. If CBDCs are to be designed with blockchain integration, careful consideration must be given to these factors to ensure that we reap the benefits of this technology without sacrificing individual rights or global financial stability.

Regulatory Oversight and Checks on Government Power

In **Chapter** 7, I outlined the legal and ethical implications of CBDCs, particularly when it comes to safeguarding personal freedoms. Here, I want to delve deeper into the kinds of **legal and institutional checks** that can prevent the abuse of a CBDC system. The introduction of a CBDC will require a legal framework that clearly defines its limits and ensures that government agencies cannot arbitrarily wield it as a tool for social control.

This could be achieved by creating **independent oversight bodies** with the power to audit the implementation and operation of CBDCs. Such bodies would need to have teeth, with the authority to hold governments and central banks accountable. In this regard, **transparency** is crucial. The public must have visibility into how the CBDC is being managed, whether through regular audits, public reports, or citizen advisory committees.

Additionally, there should be strict **limitations on data usage**. As I discussed in **Chapter 3**, the introduction of CBDCs brings with it the risk of mass surveillance, where governments could track every transaction and use this information for purposes beyond financial regulation. Laws must be enacted to ensure that the financial privacy of citizens is respected and that any data collected is strictly limited to the functions necessary for the currency's operation.

Maintaining Cash as a Backup

One of the most controversial debates surrounding CBDCs is whether physical cash should be preserved as a **backup system**. In **Chapter 6**, I touched upon the potential consequences of a digital failure, and the same concern arises here. While a purely digital system might seem efficient and modern, it is inherently vulnerable in ways that a cash-based system is not. Physical cash operates independently of the internet, electricity, or other infrastructure.

Maintaining a **hybrid system**, where physical cash remains in circulation alongside a digital currency, could offer the best of both worlds. In times of crisis be it a technical failure, natural disaster, or even political instability citizens could fall back on cash as a reliable form of payment. Some might argue that this defeats the purpose of transitioning to a digital system, but redundancy is essential when the stakes are this high.

The Role of Public Debate

Ultimately, the future of digital currencies is not something that can be dictated from the top down. As I have stressed throughout this book, and particularly in this chapter, **public discourse** is vital. The transition to a Central Bank Digital Currency (CBDC) is not just a technical decision; it is a societal one. This is why **transparency** and **citizen involvement** are paramount. Governments should not only seek expert opinion but also involve the public in discussions about how these systems are designed, implemented, and regulated.

Public debate fosters **accountability**. When citizens are aware of the risks and trade-offs, they can push back against decisions that might undermine their rights or freedoms. Moreover, informed debate can drive better policy, ensuring that the systems put in place reflect the values and priorities of the society they are meant to serve. However, for public debate to be truly effective, it must go beyond mere consultation or surface-level engagement. It requires **genuine inclusion** of diverse voices, perspectives, and communities.

A recurring theme throughout this book, from **Chapter 3's** discussion on **government control** to **Chapter 7's** exploration of **legal and ethical implications**, is the concentration of power that CBDCs potentially enable. Without public involvement, there is a danger that CBDCs could become tools of financial surveillance, as I outlined earlier, and undermine civil liberties. Public debate acts as a **counterbalance** to these risks by giving citizens a platform to challenge, question, and influence the policies surrounding CBDCs.

Importantly, **public education** plays a crucial role in this process. The technical complexities of CBDCs and the blockchain technology that could underpin them are not widely understood by the general public. Without sufficient education, the debate risks being monopolized by a few experts or political actors, leaving ordinary citizens out of the loop. To prevent this, governments and financial institutions should prioritize **financial literacy initiatives**, ensuring that the general populace is equipped to engage meaningfully in discussions about the future of money. These initiatives should explain not only the potential benefits but also the **hidden dangers** of a fully digital financial system, as I have discussed throughout this book. By empowering citizens with knowledge, we create a more informed electorate that can actively participate in shaping the direction of CBDC policies.

Additionally, **transparency** is key to fostering meaningful public debate. In **Chapter 7**, I touched upon the need for strong regulatory oversight to prevent the abuse of CBDCs. For this oversight to be effective, the process must be **transparent** and open to public scrutiny. Citizens need to see the inner workings of how decisions are made, who holds the reins of power, and what the long-term implications are for their personal freedoms and economic autonomy. **Independent media**, **academia**, and **civil society organizations** should also be involved, acting as watchdogs and providing independent analysis that can counterbalance government narratives.

Furthermore, the **diversity** of the debate matters. The implications of a cashless society will not be felt equally across different segments of society. Low-income individuals, the elderly, and those without access to reliable digital infrastructure could be disproportionately affected, as I explored in **Chapter 6** on **economic disruption and social unrest**. Public debate must include these voices, ensuring that the design of CBDCs takes into account the needs and concerns of the most vulnerable in society. Failure to do so could lead to increasing **financial exclusion**, further widening the divide between those who are digitally connected and those who are not.

Another aspect that cannot be overlooked is the role of **international public discourse**. As I discussed in **Chapter 8** on **geopolitical ramifications**, CBDCs are poised to play a significant role in global trade, cross-border payments, and financial sanctions. The implementation of a CBDC in one nation can have far-reaching consequences for other countries, particularly those that are economically dependent on larger powers. Therefore, public debate should not be confined to national borders. It must also involve international cooperation, where nations and their citizens can collectively discuss the role of CBDCs in shaping the global financial order.

In conclusion, **public debate** is not just an optional step in the process of transitioning to digital currencies it is a necessity. The introduction of CBDCs will affect every aspect of economic life, from personal privacy and financial autonomy to global power structures. Therefore, it is only right that the public plays a central role in shaping the policies and systems that will govern this transition. Without robust, transparent, and inclusive public debate, the risks of **authoritarian control**, **financial exclusion**, and **social unrest** become all the more likely. If the future of money is to be democratic, then it must be shaped by the many, not the few.

Conclusion: The Future of Money in a Digital World

Are CBDCs the inevitable evolution of money, or are they a dangerous step towards **totalitarian control**? As I have explored throughout this book, the answer lies somewhere in the middle. While there are undeniable benefits to a more digitalized financial system such as improved efficiency and transparency these must be carefully weighed against the risks. **Geopolitical tensions, cybersecurity concerns, economic disruptions**, and the **erosion of personal freedoms** are all very real dangers that we cannot ignore.

The way forward must be one of **balance**. If CBDCs are to succeed, they must be designed with **resilience, accountability, and individual rights** at their core. Safeguards must be put in place to protect against the misuse of power, and alternatives like physical cash and blockchain technology should remain in the conversation. Most importantly, the public must be an active participant in shaping the future of money, ensuring that it serves the many rather than the few.

The future of money is digital but it need not be dystopian.

Epilogue: A Reflection on Control and Chaos in a Cashless Future

As I bring this journey through the world of Central Bank Digital Currencies (CBDCs) to a close, it's clear that we stand on the precipice of a significant evolution in the way money is perceived, created, and controlled. The question that lingers is whether we are marching toward a utopia of streamlined, accessible financial systems or edging closer to a dystopia of government overreach, surveillance, and instability. What began as an exploration of the *evolution of money* from barter and coins to the digital currencies of today has morphed into a wider contemplation of power, control, and human rights in a digital age.

The Inevitability of CBDCs: Progress or Peril?

In Chapter 1, I outlined how money has constantly evolved to meet the needs of increasingly complex societies. The rise of digital transactions, cryptocurrencies, and eventually CBDCs is not just a trend but an almost inevitable development as we continue to digitise every aspect of our lives. The question, however, is not whether CBDCs will be adopted many countries are already well on their way but what kind of world they will create.

As we saw in *Chapter 2*, China's Digital Yuan serves as a prime example of how a CBDC can be weaponised for geopolitical gain and domestic control. The global interest in CBDCs is undeniable, yet the United States, the European Union, and others must carefully consider the potential for these currencies to morph into tools of oppression. The competing interests between nations could turn CBDCs into a new battleground for economic supremacy, heightening tensions and altering the balance of power on the global stage.

The Allure and Danger of Control

The ability for governments to have total financial oversight, as discussed in *Chapter 3*, introduces both benefits and significant risks. With CBDCs, the government would have visibility over every transaction, which, in theory, could help combat fraud, corruption, and illegal activities. But what happens when this visibility becomes absolute control? The very idea of *programmable money* where governments can dictate how citizens spend their own money is chilling. The loss of anonymity, as cash disappears, signals the erosion of privacy, a fundamental human right that many are not willing to trade for the sake of convenience.

Moreover, this level of control raises significant ethical concerns. *Chapter 7* highlighted how CBDCs could infringe on civil liberties, leading to a world where the government has unprecedented power over an individual's economic independence. The right to free association, privacy, and even basic financial autonomy are all at risk when money is no longer a private matter but a state-controlled entity.

Economic Fragility and Social Unrest

The potential for social and economic disruption, as outlined in *Chapter 6*, is one of the most immediate dangers posed by CBDCs. Any system reliant entirely on digital infrastructure is inherently vulnerable to failure. What happens when the digital network collapses or is hacked? The vulnerability of digital systems, explored in *Chapter 4*, means that a sophisticated cyberattack on a CBDC could lead to widespread economic paralysis, social chaos, and political upheaval. The inability to buy food, water, or necessities due to a digital currency crash is not a far-fetched nightmare it is a very real possibility. We've already seen how banking collapses and economic crises have led to riots and unrest; imagine the consequences when the currency itself is digital, vulnerable, and controlled by the few.

Geopolitical Competition and Financial Control

On a global level, the ramifications of CBDCs could fundamentally reshape international relations. *Chapter 8* examined how CBDCs could be wielded as tools of geopolitical influence, allowing nations to enforce sanctions more effectively or engage in new forms of economic warfare. Nations may use their digital currencies to influence global trade, or conversely, to isolate themselves from foreign competitors. The question of who controls cross-border payments will no longer be answered solely by the market but by governments holding digital levers of power.

The global power struggle over CBDCs is already beginning to unfold, and as nations race to establish dominance in the digital currency space, we must ask ourselves whether this competition will lead to a more efficient global economy or a fragmented world driven by digital exclusion and economic coercion.

Safeguards, Alternatives, and the Role of Public Discourse

Despite these risks, there are ways to mitigate the perils of a cashless future. *Chapter 9* offered a framework for designing resilient CBDC systems that incorporate checks and balances, regulatory oversight, and, crucially, citizen involvement. Building resilient systems is paramount. Blockchain technology, for instance, could provide a decentralised alternative or complement to centralized CBDCs, offering a layer of security and transparency that would prevent governments from wielding unchecked power over the financial system.

Moreover, maintaining physical cash as a fallback option may serve as a critical safeguard. A hybrid system where both digital and physical forms of money coexist could offer the best of both worlds: the convenience and speed of digital payments with the security and anonymity of cash. Public debate and transparency are essential in shaping the future of CBDCs. Citizens must be involved in these discussions, pushing back against overreach and ensuring that any digital currency system respects personal freedoms and autonomy.

The Future of Money: A Delicate Balance

The future of money is undoubtedly digital, but the form it takes is still very much undecided. In many ways, CBDCs are the natural evolution of money, but they are also fraught with risks that could alter the very fabric of society. Will CBDCs bring about a fairer, more inclusive financial system? Or will they give rise to an era of government surveillance and financial control on a scale never seen before?

I believe that the key lies in maintaining a delicate balance. We must embrace the benefits of technological innovation without sacrificing the rights and freedoms that define our societies. It is not enough to passively accept the march of progress; we must actively shape it. By implementing strong safeguards, promoting transparency, and fostering robust public debate, we can ensure that the digital currency revolution works for the people, not against them.

The challenge of the future is not merely technological but ethical, legal, and deeply human. How we navigate the control and chaos of a cashless world will determine whether we emerge stronger and more united or more divided and vulnerable than ever before. The decision, ultimately, lies with us.

End

Don't miss out!

Visit the website below and you can sign up to receive emails whenever John Shenton publishes a new book. There's no charge and no obligation.

https://books2read.com/r/B-A-RJUO-SAHBF

BOOKS 2 READ

Connecting independent readers to independent writers.

Did you love *Control and Chaos*? Then you should read *The Dragon's Gambit: China's Bid for Global Dominance and the Western Response*[1] by John Shenton!

[2]

In the 21st century, few challenges loom as large on the global stage as the rapid rise of China, and it's bid to assert dominance in every sphere of international influence. The Dragon's Gambit: China's Bid for Global Dominance and the Western Response provides a detailed, multifaceted exploration of this phenomenon, offering readers a critical examination of China's strategic ambitions and the global repercussions. This book does more than recount history—it dissects China's current manoeuvres, scrutinizing the far-reaching consequences and posing urgent questions for the West's response.

---

1. https://books2read.com/u/bzyZ9E

2. https://books2read.com/u/bzyZ9E

Also by John Shenton

Business Plan Basics
The Bahamas - More Islands and Recipes Than You Expect!
Collected Musings from Bricks and Mortar to E-commerce
The Smart City Odyssey: Unveiling the Secrets to Traveller-Centric
Software
The Dragon's Gambit: China's Bid for Global Dominance and the
Western Response
Silent Weapon
Business Basics: Money Sources
Influx
Fried Chips
Mandates, Motors, and Misinformation
Echos of Orwell
Control and Chaos
The Empire's Warning: What Rome's Fall Tells Us About the West
Today

About the Author

John Shenton was born in Birmingham, England and grew up in postwar England. He spent several years as a Radio Officer onboard a variety of vessels sailing to the Persian Gulf, the Indian Ocean and South China seas.

With degrees and a background in electronics and computers he has lived and worked within the United Kingdom, Germany, Switzerland and Canada.

While doing so, he established numerous trading relationships in Japan, Korea, the USA, China and other countries.

He has been retired for some time now living in Montréal Canada enjoying golfing, writing, sailing and many other things automotive.

About the Publisher

John Shenton published via Draft2digital